What Works In FASHION ADVERTISING

Interpreting the Strategic Thinking
Behind the Advertising and Communications
of Fashion Producers and Retailers

Prof. Peggy Fincher Winters / Dr. Arthur Allen Winters
and the Telefashion Group
Prof. Jeffrey Buchman and Prof. Irv Nogid

RETAIL REPORTING CORPORATION, NEW YORK

Retail Reporting Corporation
302 Fifth Avenue
New York, NY 10001

Distributors in the United States and Canada
Delmar Publications
3 Columbus Circle
Albany, NY 12212

Distributors outside the United States and Canada
Hearst Books International
1350 Avenue of the Americas
New York, NY 10019

Library of Congress Cataloging in Publication Data:
What Works in Fashion Advertising

Printed in Hong Kong
ISBN 0-934590-86-9

Book Design: Judy Shepard

ontents

Preface

WHY ANALYZE fashion advertising? Fashion ads are an indication of how producers and retailers intend to attain their marketing objectives. Their ads are examples of the tactics that help to execute their marketing or merchandising strategies.

What is a fashion advertiser's objective? It is to get consumers to prefer its brand, its service or its store over the competition. Marketing objectives are usually based on a quantitative or qualitative goal which is needed to sell products, build brands, and increase consumer loyalty.

What is an advertising strategy? It is how do you get the consumer to prefer the product, the service, the store …

To develop our analyses of advertising strategies, we have devised the **What Works Checklist,** (see Introduction, page 7). We use it throughout each of the fashion merchandise categories to interpret marketing objectives, identify the target audience, recognize positioning and appeals that build brand character, analyze creative strategies, and evaluate the tactics of copy, layout, art, graphics, and typography. Our evaluation of the tactics used in the creative execution of the message is based on the tone and theme "being on strategy."

What Works in Fashion Advertising is our attempt to share with you our process of interpreting the strategic thinking behind the advertising. However, it is by no means a typical linear process. It is an overlay for critical thinking that is indeed a *non-linear intellectual process.* We will use the checklist to identify, interpret, analyze, and critique the elements in whatever combination the advertiser's messages suggest.

Our purpose is to encourage critical thinking about what today's fashion advertising is communicating to the consumer. Each of the campaigns are selected as examples of messages that reflect a knowledge of current and emerging trends, lifestyles, and purchasing behaviors. They are placed in product categories and grouped for their value as subjects for analyses of marketing objectives, strategic positioning, brand building, and benefits that appeal to and result in consumer response.

What you will see in the following fashion categories — Men's & Women's; Children's; Accessories; Sports & Fitness; and Cosmetics & Beauty, are ads that should stimulate an inquiry into what the advertisers' objectives and strategies may have been. We hope this will add to you process of interpreting and evaluating *"what works in fashion advertising."*

The Telefashion Group:
Dr. Arthur Allen Winters
Prof. Peggy Fincher Winters
Prof. Jeffrey Buchman
Prof. Irv Nogid

How to Use *What Works in Fashion Advertising...*

WHAT WORKS IN FASHION ADVERTISING takes a provocative and critical look into what the message is communicating. Advertising that works has creative strategies and tactical executions driven by marketing objectives to build brands, sell products, and increase customer loyalty.

Fashion ads and campaigns are presented in merchandise categories and selected for what can be learned from an examination of their marketing objectives, creative strategies, and tactical executions. To survive in today's highly competitive marketplace, producers and retailers must gather and share information to better understand all aspects of consumer behavior.

Even fashion products with broad-based appeal must have separate strategies for each consumer segment. Advertisers need to know what works (and what doesn't work) to connect with the "values, attitudes, and lifestyles" that influence why, when, and where people buy.

The What Works Checklist has been devised by the editors to evaluate what works now in fashion advertising. Up to now, fashion advertising made the marketing objective fit the creative strategy—now the strategy must fit the objective. This is "being on strategy."

The *What Works Checklist* asks:

- What evidence is there that the ad's *target consumer* has been effectively profiled? Fashion consumers should be described in terms of their brand preferences and product usage, their value/price/service attitudes, lifestages, lifestyles, and shopping patterns.
- Does the ad have an *objective?* Is it clear what type of response it wants from the consumer?
- Is the strategy based on *product benefits versus consumer benefits* or both? Does the message reflect the personal positioning of the customer as well as the market positioning of the brand or store?
- How does the ad build *"brand character"?* Does it communicate the values of the brand that are most significant to the target consumer?
- Does the tactical execution of copy and art create a *"tone"* for the ad that will relate to the target consumer?
- Is there a *theme* which differentiates the brand or the store as brand from its competition?
- Refer to Key Terms used in What Works in Fashion Advertising on page 159.

"WHAT WORKS ... " offers a way of interpreting the strategic thinking behind the advertising and communications of fashion producers and retailers.

WHAT WORKS IN

Men's & Women's

FASHION

ADVERTISING

Advertising strategy often focuses on identifying the product's "U.S.P." But in this case we recognize that Barneys is not presenting the "Unique Selling Proposition" of the product, as much as it has chosen to establish a "Unique Selling Personality" for their stores.

Barneys' objective is to build recognition for its featured brand names and to increase equity for its store as a brand. The store is positioned as a fashion-forward institution for the fashion cognoscenti. The quality is high and so are the prices.

The ads use quips and one-liners to connect with a sophisticated upscale customer. The copy is conversational enough to be what he or she might say—or even be the subject of … The creative strategy is to send a message about Barneys' fashion knowledge and authority. The singular quotes and unorthodox representation of the clothing communicates something special to New York's fashion customers.

Other stores may feature the same designers, but Barneys suggests that they have deeper insights into the designers' philosophies. It also suggests that Barneys will know what is most appropriate and interesting for their customers' wardrobes.

This store's campaign takes a confident stand to differentiate itself with such an identifiable style of art. (This artist's work has also been used by Saab in its TV campaign.)

BARNEYS
NEW YORK

Hair by Roger Thompson Salon

Millie had a way of bringing out the beast in Kurt.

Millie and Kurt are wearing
Giorgio Armani

BARNEYS
NEW YORK

Hair by Roger Thompson Salon

Pierre talked to dolphins. Ray ignored them.

Pierre is wearing
t-shirt, sport coat, trousers and
jacket by Barneys New York.

Ray is wearing shirt,
sweater and trousers by
Barneys New York
sport coat by Redaelli

BARNEYS
NEW YORK

Hair by Roger Thompson Salon

Ruth had multiple personalities. They all had credit cards.

Ruth is wearing
jacket and pants by Jil Sander
makeup by Look

In addition to compelling attention with its eye-catching "art class" graphics, this campaign recognizes a specific consumer segment in the Levi's "jeans for women" market. Their first campaign used abstract artists' renderings to introduce the new product category—"jeans for women" and its own "W" logo to a demographically older female target market.

This campaign creates its own "voice" by using "girl-speak." The layout's use of color and creative hand-lettering differentiates this campaign from the older consumer segment. It positions itself against its main competitor (Lee, "The Brand That Fits.")

The strategy is calculated to appeal to women who want to look as good as the guys in their jeans. Hence the product is described as "guy's fitting"… but with design and fit attributes which recognize "the way you curve." Levi's makes use of their estimable brand equity by assuring the customer—"But all the good stuff (what the guy's jeans have), stays the same."

We feel that the double spread ad is the most effective in giving women a reason to buy. The jeans are on a woman, just doing it—fitting better than her boyfriend's … (although who could tell the difference except for the curves rendered in above the waistline).

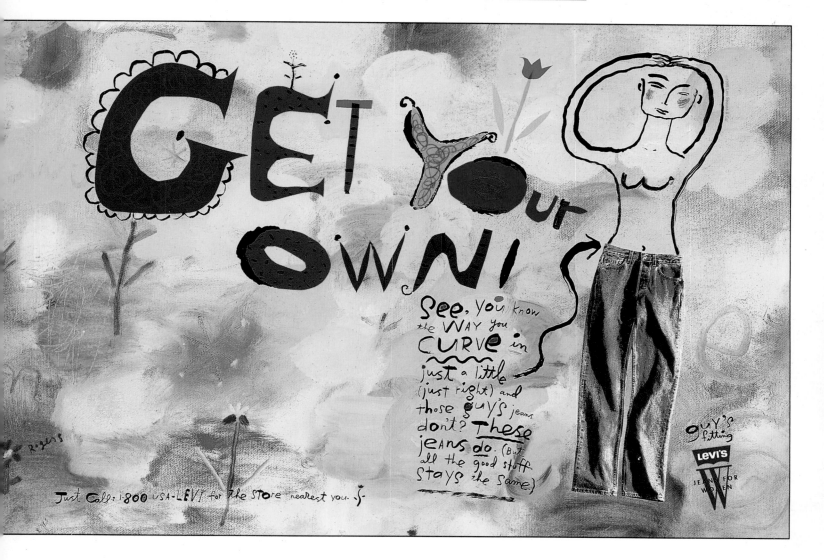

SHAUNA STEIN
Los Angeles, CA

SUSAN
San Francisco, CA

RAZOOKS
Greenwich, CT

Cheap and Chic by

MOSCHINO

Does anyone really believe that fashion producers can help the world become more socially responsible? We have seen Benetton, Moschino, and now Joop adopt this I-am-a-company-that-cares positioning strategy. It's a way of differentiating their company from the competition, those "bottom-liners" whose sole interest is to sell something!

Even if we accept that the key objective in their campaign is to appeal to I-care-about-the-society motivations—can we now believe that this is the best way to sell the product?

Let's compare the appeals of these two campaigns by Joop and Moschino …

Joop Jeans is presenting "Jest A Thought," with power headlines and eye-catching visuals, in each of its ads. They speak to a consumer segment of the jeans and sportswear market who may be tired of anorexic models (e.g. Calvin Klein). Joop is seeking to build brand-name recognition through "deep thoughts" and intriguing photography. These ads draw the reader in and ask them to stop and think about the "idea" and to remember that Joop thinks about more than just jeans.

Moschino is stepping away from its social indictment messages to a playful play on words. But what is "cheap or chic" about these fashions? There is no real believable information about price or quality other than the statement made by the slogan and the logo. Must we assume that the customer knows the Moschino collection and is familiar with its "chic"? But what does "cheap" mean?

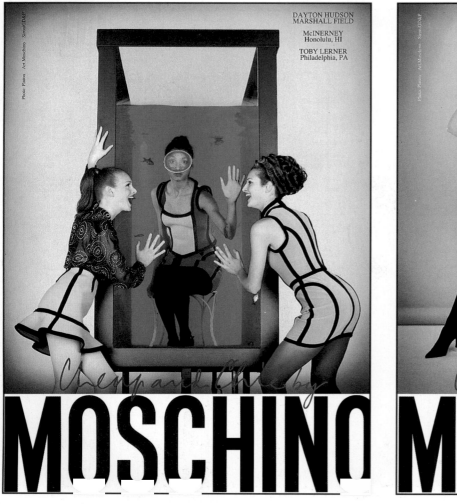

DAYTON HUDSON
MARSHALL FIELD

McINERNEY
Honolulu, HI

TOBY LERNER
Philadelphia, PA

Cheap and Chic by

MOSCHINO

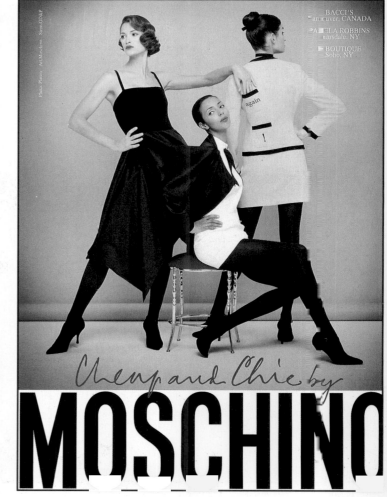

BACCI'S
Vancouver, CANADA

ANGELA ROBBINS
Scarsdale, NY

BOUTIQUE
Soho, NY

Cheap and Chic by

MOSCHINO

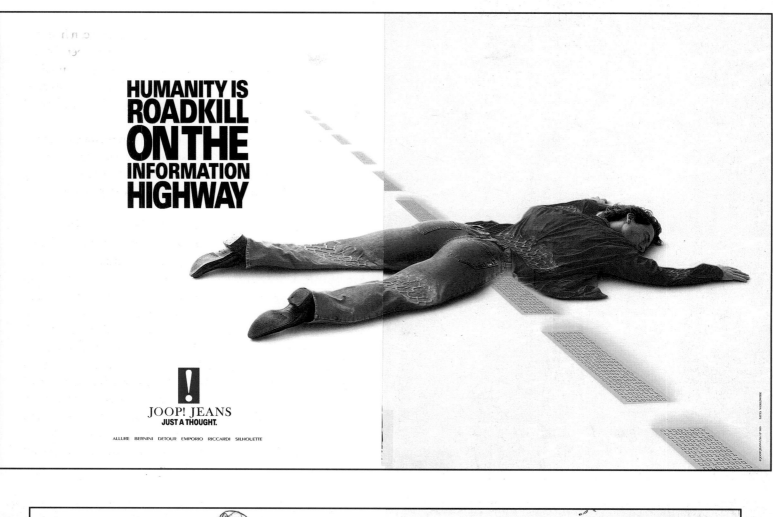

The simple black dress always makes an elegant fashion statement. Note the grace of the curved line of copy that accentuates the new touch on Dolce & Gabbana's soft drape-back dress. The monochromatic photography lends importance to Louis of Boston's visual/verbal fashion message.

The selling of elegance takes on a bolder approach in this Hermes' western landscape. Notice their "Hermes 1995 Year of the Road" symbol. It indicates this collection's inspiration, and the campaign's connection to a new take on traditional images. The copy "Time Makes the Difference," implies that Hermes is now interpreting classic international looks for today's global markets.

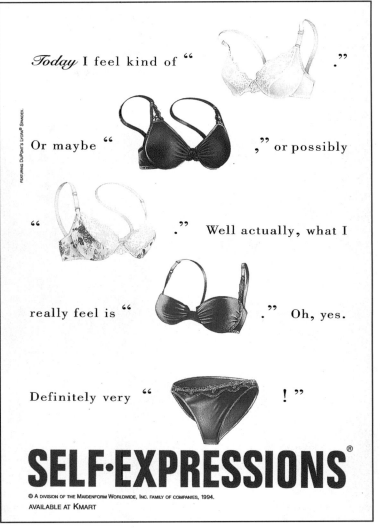

SELF·EXPRESSIONS®

© A DIVISION OF THE MAIDENFORM WORLDWIDE, INC. FAMILY OF COMPANIES, 1994.
AVAILABLE AT KMART

Today I feel kind of " ." Or maybe " ," or possibly " ." Well actually, what I really feel is " ." Oh, yes. Definitely very " ! "

Cotton so cosy it's like being in a cocoon.

It *may* be a detail *but* it's a Chantelle

Cannelle by Chantelle

·Paris · New York · Tokyo · Montréal·

NEIMAN MARCUS   I. MAGNIN   SAKS FIFTH AVENUE   NORDSTROM SAN FRANCISCO

Is the objective of these bra and lingerie ads to sell product benefits, reinforce brand image or help the consumer to create a self-image? All three of these objectives are demonstrated by the art and copy in these three ads. Chantelle focuses on product attributes of cotton fabric and the product benefits of styling "cosy" enough to offer a "cocoon" instead of a cleavage.

Maidenform's "Self Expressions" uses the emotional-bond-with-the-consumer approach. The ad's tone suggests that it understands how she feels and has the product that fits each feeling.

Ritratti attempts to develop brand character by being very Italian and offers an "Italian Portrait" for self-image. Typically Italian, it uses words and body language to send its sexy message.

THE ITALIAN PORTRAIT OF LINGERIE.

RITRATTI

NEIMAN MARCUS
Beverly Hills, CA.

NORDSTROM
Skokie, IL.

SAMANTHA JONES LINGERIE
New York, N.Y. (212) 308 6680

NANCY MEYER
Seattle, WA. (206) 625 5552

PERLISSIMA AT THE PLAZA
New York, N.Y. (212) 308 7904

ADELE & AGNES
Englewood, N.J. (201) 568 4949

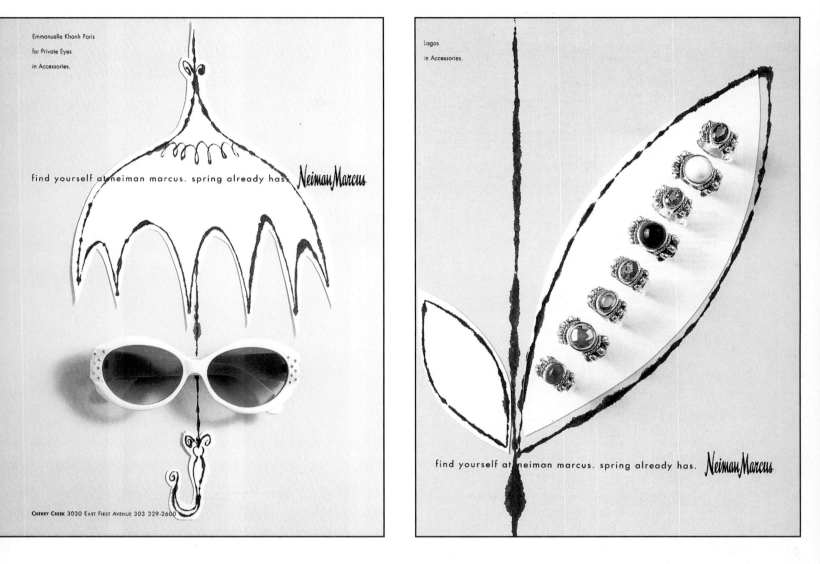

Emmanuelle Khanh Paris
for Private Eyes
in Accessories.

find yourself at neiman marcus. spring already has. *Neiman Marcus*

CHERRY CREEK 3030 EAST FIRST AVENUE 303 329-2600

Logos
in Accessories.

find yourself at neiman marcus. spring already has. *Neiman Marcus*

Retailers may gain status from the designer apparel and accessories they carry in their stores and feature in their ads, but each retailer must establish their own unique image. In order to stand out from the crowd, each of these stores has created a style that will differentiate it from its competition.

Nordstrom has chosen the most traditional layout style known in advertising: symmetrical, formal balance. The ad is designed with a strong "picture frame" with centered photo and the logo centered in the lower third. Dominance is the goal and it is achieved in this campaign. The product takes center stage, while the designer and store identities are given proper theatrical billing. The copy is briefly informative and does more to sell the target consumer on the idea that Nordstrom is the place for "Fashion genius..." and "Very, very extraordinary..." merchandise.

The store with the most consistent style over the years is Lord and Taylor with their "The Signature of American Style". While Nordstrom gave top billing to its chosen designers, Lord &

Taylor's strategy is to provide their own fashion advice, using the designer's name (in light face type in the body copy) and merchandise to represent their point. Their other key message is the personal shopping service, The Red Rose Service, with its 1-800 number. The signature rose completes the corporate image and unique identity mark.

Neiman Marcus combines illustrated graphic cutouts with actual products in a composed photograph. Distinctiveness is a key to being noticed by the readers of magazines, the reader must be given a reason to stop flipping the pages and "read" this ad! Neiman Marcus has a variety of campaigns running at one time to communicate its institutional messages and promote its different merchandise departments. The accessories category is being featured in this spring campaign. The strategy is to express the idea that the target consumer should — "find yourself at neiman marcus. spring already has."—to be in style with the newest spring fashions, the consumer must go to Neiman Marcus — now! This is suggestive, seasonal selling in print.

PUT OUR JEANS ON

GAP DENIM

These three Gap campaigns are an excellent example of how a company needs to develop a distinctly dedicated strategy for each of their brands and/or merchandise categories. Baby Gap's campaign strategy is to show the parent-as-customer that The Gap understands baby lifestyles. The ads develop a tone that relates to the customer by recognizing that it's never too early to suit up for self-idealization — as a flower child — or as a budding olympian for the crawl event.

The Gap Denim and the Authentic Gap Footwear ads have the same objective. The denim ad's objective is an attempt to compete in a major category that is dominated by the competition — Levi's, Lee, et al.... The objective in the footwear ad is to inform the Gap fan club that Gap now has a category — really authentic sneakers (like they used to be before the Nike make-overs).

Gap goes back to its origins with its Gap denim. Again they create a tone of the "real thing" — by focusing on one of denimwear's features, their metal button — of course engraved with the Gap logo and the year of their birth, 1969.

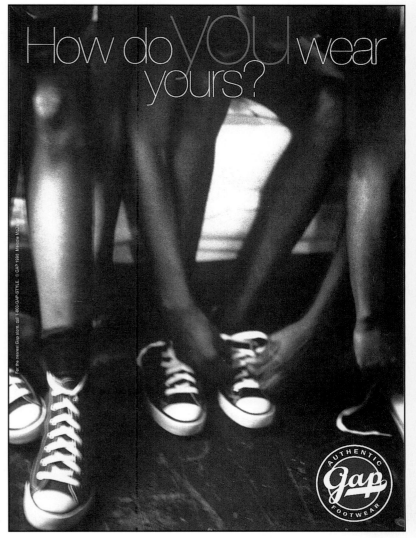

How do you wear yours?

Gap
AUTHENTIC FOOTWEAR

THE LIZGOLF COLLECTION FOR SPRING 1996

your game
NEVER LOOKED BETTER
LIZGOLF BY LIZ CLAIBORNE

macy's

CALL MACY'S BY APPOINTMENT FOR DETAILS: 212-494-4181. OUTSIDE NEW YORK, 1-800-343-0121.

"Come see the softer side of Sears" is much more than a slogan. It is a statement of repositioning that sends a message not only to the consumer but to all who do business with this retail giant. The objective is to describe a change in their retail system and merchandise mix that is more than spin-deep. Their strategy in these two ads is clear. For example, the dryer... (they still want to sell hard goods) is featured in order to deliver a play-on-words that focus on the soft goods of fashion.

We doubt if Macy*s New York has a significant segment of women customers who are golfers... outside of New York, maybe. In either case, this must be part of Macy's strategy. As per their recently announced objective to reinvent their store, they are changing their merchandise mix with less emphasis on price.

Featuring the "Lizgolf" collection by Liz Claiborne may be part of their repositioning strategy. This double spread may sell the Lizgolf collection... the prices are substantially lower than in the pro shops. But what does it do for the store? Macy's has done nothing in this advertisement to send their message, other than place the logo on the green.

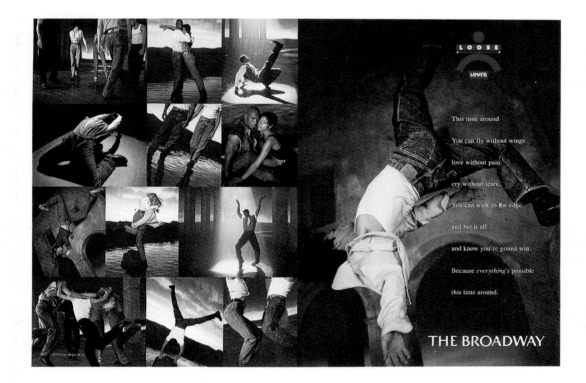

This time around

You can fly without wings

love without pain

cry without tears.

You can walk to the edge

and bet it all

and know you're gonna win.

Because *everything's* possible

this time around.

THE BROADWAY

How loose can you be in defining "loose"? Here Levi's attempts two approaches — one visual and one verbal. The flag bearer wears the product, standing loosely in silhouette, with flaring flag and blouse-y jeans. The visual message asks the consumer to identify with the feelings and spirit of those who can "loosen up".

The Broadway ad does it with verse-like copy and visual quick-cuts of product that attempt to persuade that "everything's possible" if your jeans this time around are Levi's — and loose. Does this mean that tight jeans prevent "love without pain"?

The "Lee Fit Check" is one of a campaign that uses a double spread to emphasize brand benefits. The strategy is to demonstrate product attributes and performance. Lee jeans are visualized in a series of tasks that consumers in their target market know all too well. These two ads seem to suggest that if the jeans fit, the jobs of moving and painting will seem like fun? The message is — the "brand that fits" not only looks good, but works good.

Woman trusting her instincts.

Does Levi's still feel that women need to be told who they are, what they can do and what they may feel? Apparently this Levi's Jeans for Women ad believes in the Virginia Slims-like strategy that sends a we-support-your-gender identity message.

These three "W" ads use a variety of compelling and esthetically effective visuals. The copy one-liners are designed to create a tone that connects with a woman's feelings about herself — "listening to her heart and trusting her instincts," as well as her relationships with others — "not taking no for an answer" — from whom? This campaign is evidently targeted to a consumer segment who Levi's believes is more interested in how the maker relates to them than how the garment is made, how it fits and how it looks.

When one considers the entire portfolio of brands in the Levi's stable, one can see how each brand is given an independent image through its advertising, while maintaining the overall institutional Levi's character.

Often, the problems in a person's life can be traced to one pivotal event during childhood. Don't buy your kid the wrong shorts.

These days, conventional wisdom has it that even a slight miscalculation in child-rearing can have lasting impact on a kid's life. That puts parents in a tough spot.

Why, your kid might do something wrong someday and blame you because you're the one who made him eat his peas. Worse yet, he might grow up to be real successful, and then write one of those tell-all books about how you were once ten minutes late picking him up from his trumpet lesson.

Considering all this, would you really want to risk buying your kid the wrong pair of shorts? Just imagine walking into a room twenty years from now and overhearing your daughter saying, ". . . and it's all because she dressed me funny."

Lee Shorts might be your safest alternative. They're designed to fit kids perfectly, and look good enough to keep moms and dads out of trouble. In fact, there's a large variety of stylish Lee Shorts to choose from. So the chances that you'll bring home a pair your child will actually wear are really quite good.

Better yet, bring the youngsters along, and let them pick out a suitable pair of Lee Shorts themselves. This not only reduces your liability in possible future litigation, but also might allow your children to have some fun.

Which will be good practice for them, since a pair of shorts from Lee has occasionally been known to bring out the kid in a kid.

Lee
The brand that fits.

You took dad's advice about women. You took dad's advice about money. Don't make the same mistake with shorts.

Whoever coined the phrase 'father knows best' probably was not talking about Pop's expertise in selecting a wardrobe. What young man, after all, hasn't cringed at the sight of the family patriarch wearing his Sunday worst?

Especially since Dad always seemed to save his most ridiculous ensembles for the front lawn, whose noxious dose of applied chemical fumes was the only explanation for a grown man wearing stripes, checks and polka dots at the same time.

And the shorts. Who on earth bought those things? They were so bad the old fella could offend passersby even without taking his shirt off.

It was enough to turn a lot of young guys away from the idea of donning a pair of shorts altogether. That is, until they discovered an alternative; Lee Shorts.

Lee makes shorts that are designed to make men look good. They're comfortable. They're very stylish. And they don't come equipped with those little white belts.

What's more, Lee Shorts fit you every bit as well as your favorite pair of Lee Jeans does. So they don't ride up under your armpits the way Dad's did.

And here's more good news. Lee Shorts are available in a variety of fits and styles, including Relaxed Fit, Loose Fit, and even new Wrinkle-Resistant 100% Cotton Casuals.

Which means that no matter how many discouraging thoughts linger on about the kind of shorts your dad used to wear, Lee can help you take comfort in one simple truth. Your wardrobe doesn't have to be hereditary.

Lee
The brand that fits.

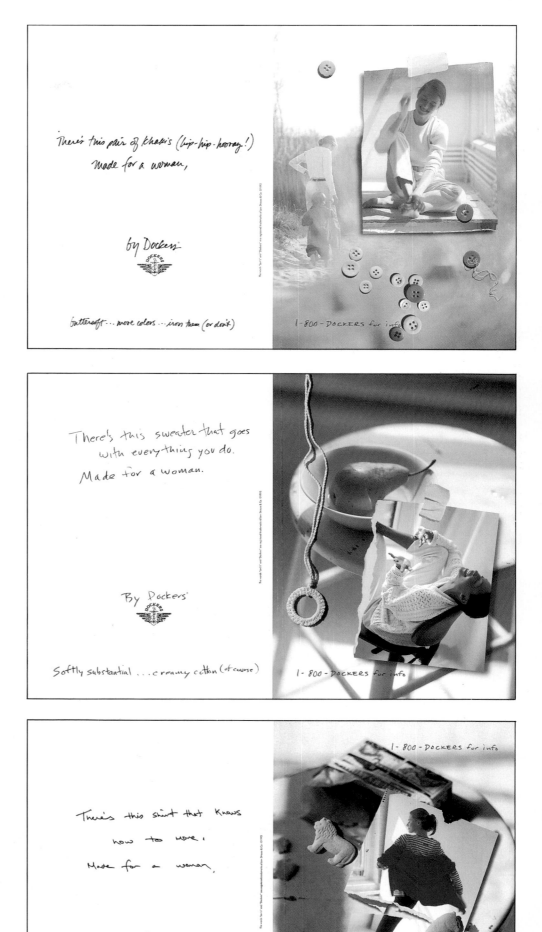

What is Lee saying about parents in their offering of advice to consumers?

These two ads from their "brand that fits" campaign series feature visuals and copy that are appealing and readable. There is no problem in seeing the product benefit differences between the Lee shorts and the "wrong shorts". The photo visuals of the "right shorts" and the insets of their category variations, "regular," "relaxed," and "loose" fit, present significant values and attributes of the Lee brand to the consumer. But what is the tone of the hidden message in the narrative copy? Do I need to be reminded how silly my father looked — or how easy it is for a parent to make a mistake in selecting anything for today's I-am-old-before-my- time kids?

The Docker's campaign also offers advice to the consumer. The strategy here is to send a clear message in a woman's voice about casual dressing for her own lifestyle. Each ad features a Dockers product with copy that contains wardrobe counseling. Visuals are enhanced by montaged symbols of the various lifestyles that are "made for a woman".

MANY A SUCCESSFUL MAN

HAS LOST HIS SHIRT.

NO DRAWER IS SAFE if it contains the legendary cotton oxford from
Brooks. Decisively rated the best of its kind, it is the single most
sought-after item in the Brooks Brothers wardrobe. At $48, it is worth
buying in quantity as a hedge against unauthorized use. Other dress
shirts, in an A-to-Z of colors, collars and patterns, are priced from $38.
For store locations or a catalog, please call 1-800-274-1816.

Brooks Brothers
CLOTHING
ESTABLISHED 1818

AT HOME ANYWHERE IN THE WORLD.

NEW YORK 212-421-4488 • COSTA MESA 714-444-1534
WILKES BASHFORD • BOYD'S • LOUIS • NEIMAN MARCUS • M.PENNER • HARRY ROSEN • ULTIMO

Ermenegildo Zegna

The objective in each of these four ads is to position their brand... Zegna, a designer brand... Brooks Brothers, the store-as-a-brand... Savane, a national brand and Callaway, a private label brand.

The tone in all four is based on the frame of reference of each of the targeted consumer segments. Brooks Brothers uses the unisex appeal of their "legendary Oxford shirt" to position their store as a wardrobe authority.

Ermenegildo Zegna wants to position himself as a designer for the global man. The whimsical visual shows a fireman's red jacket and ensemble "at home" in a fireman's closet — spotted there with a fire dog. The headline reflects the objective and strategy that the product will work "anywhere in the world".

Did Callaway consider how the golfer's "intelligence and strength" might react to the lovely shot of the golf course focusing on a water trap? Certainly the sophisticated copy and art are designed to appeal to the golfer's eye and inner ear. The colors in the golf course are effectively coordinated to the colors in the shirt. The objective is to position Callaway as a specialist in golf apparel — a specialist who also understands the mind of the golfer.

The Savane ad is one of a campaign whose strategy is to position the brand with a strong association to "No Wrinkle". Here they reinforce the attributes of their product with a series of quick-cuts "from a different cloth". The consumer is confronted with reasons-to-buy that range from: quality construction, color selection, value-pricing and easy-care... to promises of looking better in the pants than your father. The disclaimer that Savane's single-stitching cannot provide an eczema-seborrhea-psoriasis defense may be trying too hard for a laugh.

Appearances can be deceiving, but you can trust the wool that wears the WOOLMARK

PURE NEW WOOL No matter how you look at it, wool drapes well, sheds wrinkles and turns heads. For more information c 11 800-986-WOOL.

These three ads basically may represent what "has been" in fashion advertising — the fashion model in front of a fashion photographer. The Woolmark ad attempts to deliver a message about the quality and performance of wool — but we believe it misses the mark with its distracting visual and ineffective typographical layout. Do you trust "wool that wears the Woolmark" to turn heads or "behead" them? How about a visual that supports the product's attributes of draping well and shedding wrinkles?

Herve Leger presents — computer-generated models who look great enough to hate. They are posed in fashions that fit too well not to be computer-aided fitting. The art direction and production however are very effective in presenting the fantasy of fashion. The strategy is to have the models "voice" and style send the designer's message from Paris.

BCBG Paris... New York, Beverly Hills, and San Francisco, positions itself as a seductive seller. The posing of the model works well with the short copy narrative that suggests what can happen to whatever you wear. The strategy is to promise consumer benefits that happen in the bedroom, perhaps as a consequence of giving someone a BCBG gift after a long absence?

HERVE LEGER, 29, RUE DU FAUBOURG SAINT HONORE, 75008 PARIS, TEL: 011 33 1 44 51 57 17

PHOTO INEZ VAN LAMSWEERDE & VINOODH MATADIN

HERVE
LEGER
PARIS

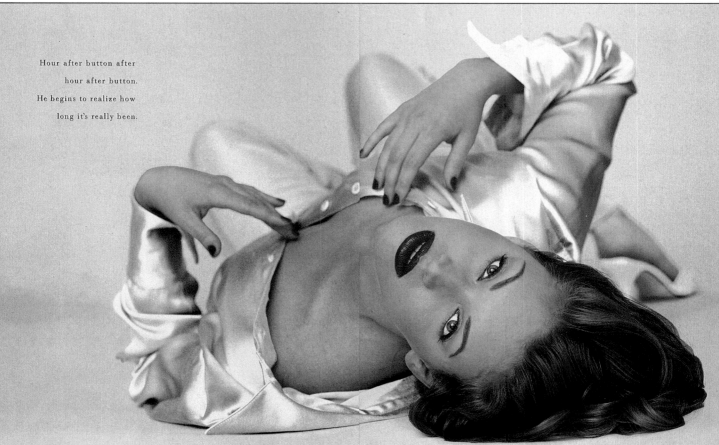

Hour after button after
hour after button.
He begins to realize how
long it's really been.

B.C.B.G. Paris

B.C.B.G. New York · Beverly Hills · San Francisco

THE ART OF FASHION

PHOTOGRAPHY BY GEOF KERN

SOME DAY I'LL BE A FAMOUS FASHION MODEL AND WEAR BEAUTIFUL CLOTHES

NeimanMarcus

BADGLEY MISCHKA

BILL BLASS

NeimanMarcus

THIERRY MUGLER

NeimanMarcus

These Neiman-Marcus ads on the "Art of Fashion" start with a credit that recognizes more of the art of the fashion photographer than of the fashion designer. This suggests that the N-M objective is to position its store as a significant patron of the art of fashion.

We are somewhat confused by the tone. The line of copy is coming from (what appears to be) a 16-year old girl. She is dreaming of becoming "a famous fashion model so that she can wear beautiful clothes". What is the profile of the audience for this message? How does a very young model's fantasy relate to the Neiman's core customer? Do their customers have to be fashion models to wear such beautiful clothes?

The photography is dramatic and is very effective — it involves the eye and the mind with its off-beat situations, its mannequin-like models, and its real mannequins.

We believe that this collection of retail ads — each featuring a prominent designer — could be a good example of cooperative advertising. The objective is to position Neiman Marcus as a store that has a special appreciation for great fashion and its designers — as well as a unique showcase for the presentation of their original creations.

New York City is a nice place to visit — but would you want to dress like you lived there? Donna Karan's DKNY collection is positioned as New York City fashion. Note the NYC reverse knock-out on the DKNY logo, and the location shoots on the streets of the city that set the tone.

The strategy is to position DKNY as a wardrober for a city person — or a city wannabe — in New York, or any other major metropolis, here or abroad. The effective juxtaposition of DK and NY indicates that this is right on target.

About half of the world now lives in cities. And for the segment of those populations who can afford to and want to, DKNY is their designer. Their individual design is to be city-oriented.

The retail ads for Louis, Boston are traditional fashion advertising — soft-sell identification of a store with a designer brand. What the Louis Woman ad seems to convey is that Louis Boston also sells women's designer fashions. The double spread for Donna Karan's men's has the same objective — but its visual message is more successful in relating to its customer segment.

SUIT BY DRIES VAN NOTEN, BELGIUM. LOUIS,BOSTON. 234 BERKELEY STREET. 1 800 225 5135

Louis, Woman.

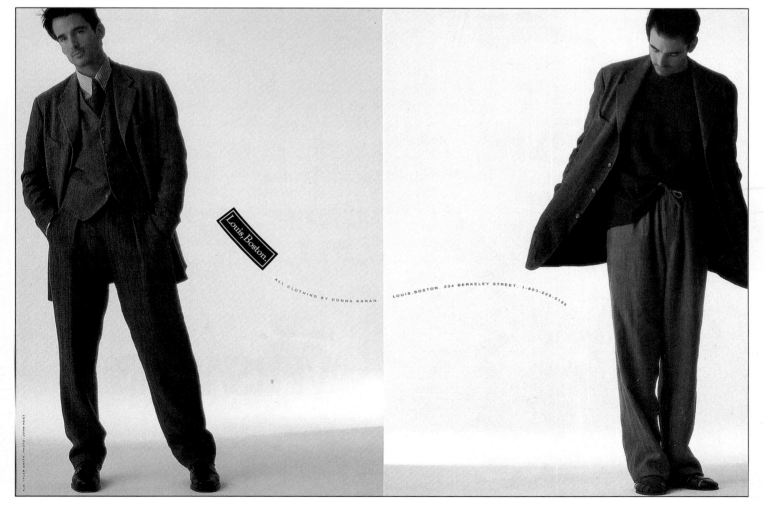

Louis, Boston.

ALL CLOTHING BY DONNA KARAN.

LOUIS,BOSTON. 234 BERKELEY STREET. 1-803-225-5135

Express Handknitted Provencale Sweater, $60
Hand-Pleated Silk Shirt, $78

EXPRESS
TRICOT
Fine Knit Clothing In The French Tradition

Compagnie Internationale
EXPRESS

The Express Tricot Collection is available exclusively at Express Stores.
To find out how to open an Express Credit Card Account,
or for the Express Store nearest you, please call 1-800-726-3200.

© 1993 Express

Here are two different approaches to the concept of fashion as a globalized product. Compagnie Internationale Express is one of the Limited's store groups that the advertiser feels has the potential to be a global brand. Even though the Limited has not expanded overseas significantly, this ad's objective is to build the store's brand character as a "compagnie internationale". The strategy is to position itself as exclusive in the moderate price range with fashions "in the French tradition".

The photograph, the look of the model, and the French-style interior design try to persuade us with eye-filling detail of rich color, sumptuous tricot, and lavish styling. The strategy is to reflect the mood and movement to international fashion.

Hermès Paris is truly an international group with stores in posh places in the U.S., France, Mexico, and Canada. The photography and the product information copy bespeak (rather than sing) that elegant fashion is "on the road again". Willie Nelson is nowhere to be seen — but Hermès creates a unique tone that suggests this is "the year of the road" for its dramatic international fashion.

IF YOU'RE DYING TO SPEND A LOT OF MONEY, COME ON IN. WE'LL GLADLY RECOMMEND AN EXPENSIVE RESTAURANT.

Hit or Miss
S·T·O·R·E·S

For a store near you, call 1-800-94-STYLE.
Style and color shown is representative of our selection.

Pantsuit with velvet detail, under $60.

THE ONLY DRAWBACK IS, IT COULD MAKE EVERYTHING ELSE IN YOUR CLOSET LOOK REALLY, REALLY OVERPRICED.

Hit or Miss
S·T·O·R·E·S

For a store near you, call 1-800-94-STYLE.
Styles and colors shown are representative of our selection.

Jumpsuit priced under $60.

TELL YOUR FRIENDS YOU PAID LESS THAN $50 A BLAZER. YOU'LL EITHER IMPRESS THEM OR ANNOY THEM COMPLETELY.

Hit or Miss
S·T·O·R·E·S

For a store near you, call 1-800-94-STYLE.

Pure wool blazers in a variety of stunning colors.

ACT CASUAL WHEN YOU SEE THE PRICETAG. YOU CAN HOOT WHEN YOU GET IN THE DRESSING ROOM.

Hit or Miss
S·T·O·R·E·S

For a store near you, call 1-800-94-STYLE.
Styles and colors shown are representative of our selection.

The season's latest style, entire outfit under $85.

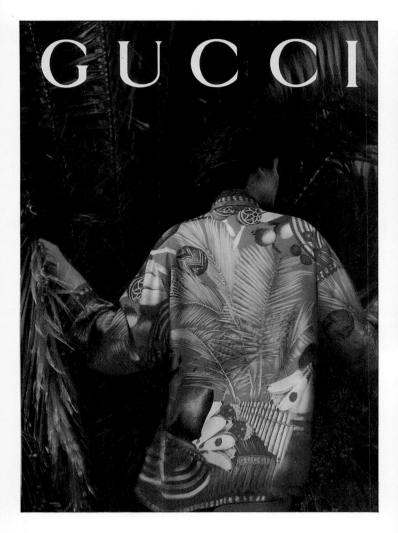

What a contrast between these two campaigns! Hard-sell vs. Soft-sell. The Hit or Miss Stores campaign gets right to the point. Their objective is to convince the value-for-a-price customer that they just can't miss getting unbeatable value in a "store near you" (call 1-800-94 STYLE).

The strategy is to give the customer the satisfaction of hanging "a real buy" in her own closet. The layout, art, copy are designed to provide instant recognition. How many fashion ads can leave out their logos and still be recognized? Cover up the Gucci in their ads — and even the fashion cognoscenti might fail to identify the advertiser...

The Gucci ads may be too soft-sell for today's skeptical and information-hungry customer. They are fashion shots — but really, what is their message? The quality of the photography may exemplify the quality of Gucci collections, but is Gucci the only resource for beautiful fashion for beautiful people? What is their basis for differentiation? How about giving the ads a theme based on a knowledge of the activities of their consumer segments? How about developing a positioning strategy to differentiate the character of the brand from its competition?

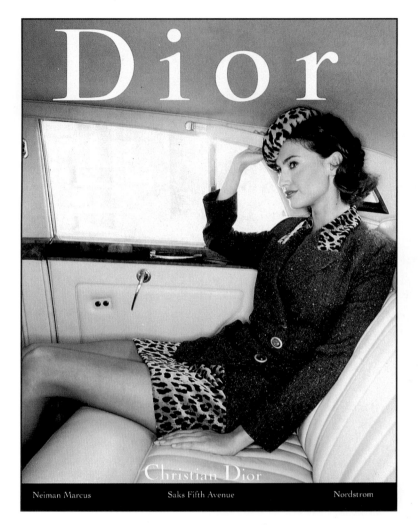

Here's more of the same old stuff in fashion advertising. Try switching the logos on each of these three campaigns and see what you get. Unless you know that the model in the ad below is really Isaac Mizrahi himself — and you recognize members of the Dior and Gucci families in their ads, you are nowhere.

All kidding aside — these ads are crafted by experienced photographers and advertising designers. They are competent and certainly create a tone designed to get some positive response from their upscale target market. But is the name of the designer always enough to position the brand against competition? We suggest that you refer to the Barney's campaign that does have an identifiable strategy, a theme based on consumer segment behavior, and a relevant tone and message.

GUCCI

ISAAC MIZRAHI

Available at Bloomingdale's, New York

GIRLS

GIRLS' FIT RED TAB 597.

It's hard to tell from the Pepe Jeans and Levi's ads exactly what is their message. The strategy is obvious — let's talk the language of our consumer segment — and let's talk about social issues that concern our audience. Pepe Jeans creates a tone that indicates that their strategy regards shock value as a component of brand value.

Is Levi's really interested in the "transvestjeans" market? The gratuitous appeals, sleazy approach, and rough tone in these two campaigns are modeled after Guess Jeans and Benetton. We suspect that this genre has run its course.

Jean Paul Gaultier's ad uses a dynamic layout, art and graphics to take the consumer on an exciting fashion trip. This ad is a journey into the creative imagination of the fashion designer. His art and craft is exemplified in products inspired by the wonderful world of costume design. It is evident that Gaultier wants to demonstrate his historical design research and his talent for using exotic fabrics and decoration. He provides the reader with a unique visual experience, that also serves to differentiate his brand.

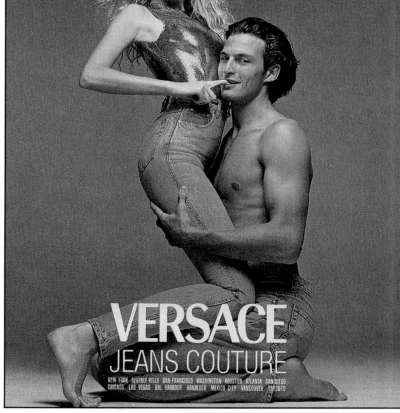

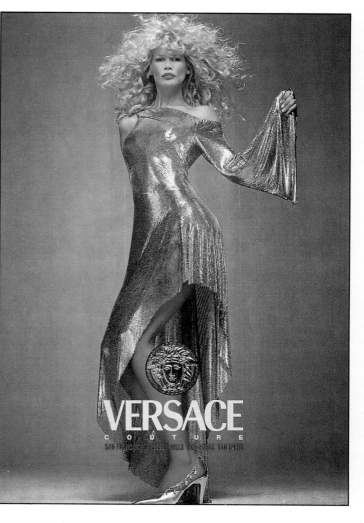

Gianni Versace! A world-class celebrity designer's advertising needs to send a special message. The theme and tone in these Versace ads are no doubt inspired by the Italian sculptor's fascination with the human form (...though Michelangelo might not have appreciated the finger in the mouth move... he certainly would recognize "the Pieta" in red).

Versace's fashions are made visually expositive by the fashion photographer's art. Versace's objective is to show to his world-wide upscale fans his skill with fabric, line, and detail... to show his "Versacetility" with any category, from Jeans (notice even they are "couture"), to sportswear, to the most dramatic, "drop-dead" special occasion gala wear.

The strategy is not to shock but to delight the eye and the mind with exquisite form and tactile texture — from bare skin to glistening lamé. Sort of makes you want to prance...

These two Diesel ads present two very different societal groups and offer "Successful Living" guides for "people interested in general health and mental power". There's also a number you can call the "U.S. Diesel Team" for more philosophy on "People, Health, and Power".

"So what if he's not young anymore? Just close your eyes, take a deep breath and go for gold!" Is this advice (in very small print below the stuffed briefs of the Golden Boys) for Diesel's consumer segment of "working girls" who want to know "how to make love pay"?

The "Ozzie and Harriet" and "Leave it to Beaver" style ad for Diesel sounds like a political ad on family values from the religious right. "Do you know that your children (and yourself) are being brainwashed every day...???" Is the objective to bond with their audience who have the same response to present-day pundits of morality? More probable, the strategy is to send-up a social spoof that is memorable enough to come up in the consumer's conversation, and to build brand recognition.

The Jean Paul Gaultier ad is another statement by the designer that he is a costume historian who appreciates the contribution to his art made by the diverse societies and cultures that make up his planet.

Those who think nature is hostile have never stepped into Kenzo's world.

KENZO
Creations for a more beautiful world.
Kenzo - 805 Madison Avenue - New York - NY 10021.

Kenzo recalled that some creatures use all their powers of attraction to capture their prey.

KENZO
Creations for a more beautiful world.
Kenzo - 805 Madison Avenue - New York - NY 10021.

NICE SHOT.

NO STORE on earth has lived your weekend passions like Brooks. Decades of experience went into this mesh shirt. Sure, it's $38 but will more than likely outlive your handicap. Ditto the $55 cotton shorts–which may even outlast your lucky iron. Both shirt & shorts get better with time. Can any golfer say the same? For the store nearest you, or a copy of our catalog, call 1-800-274-1815.

One of the most effective strategies for developing loyal and lasting fashion customers is to communicate values that bond the consumer to the designer. For whatever reason — self-idealization, celebrity, quality or value — the growing group of global designers have the same objective: to create a world-wide fan club by positioning themselves through a differentiation of philosophy.

In this Kenzo campaign — the designer draws upon his Japanese roots and his country's belief that nature is the world's most creative designer. The strategy is to present Kenzo's fashion "creations for a more beautiful world," side by side with his not-quite-Haiku observations on nature.

The Brooks Brothers campaign has an institutional rather than product objective. It attempts to position itself as a fashion authority, guide and advisor. The featured men's and women's apparel is described in values that evidently demonstrate an understanding of their customers. The photography creates a tone that helps the reader to recreate an experience in which the apparel may play an important part. The copy is informative soft-sell. It is reinforced by an invitation to learn more about the store by calling a 1-800 phone number.

BROOKS.
IN NEUTRAL.

THE FEEL of a favorite piece of clothing. It's something very familiar to women who wear Brooks Brothers. From the drape of the sandwashed silk and the understated details comes the kind of comfort that leaves you entirely at ease. Whether the whole world is watching–or you've left it all behind. (Jacket, $145. Trousers, $95.) For the store nearest you, or a copy of our catalog, call 1-800-274-1816.

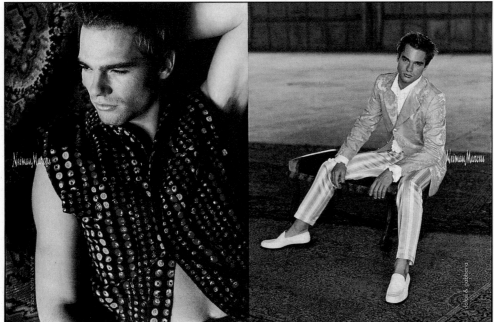

How does a store establish itself in the consumer's mind as a fashion authority? To satisfy this objective Neiman Marcus uses a series of pages in Gentleman's Quarterly to describe "the art of dressing" and illustrate the process by serving as a wardrobe consultant to this guy. Even though he has the unshaved "Brad Pitt look" throughout, Neiman's uses the product to make him look different enough to suggest that he leads multiple lives. The strategy is to position N-M as an upscale men's specialty store plus — as being capable of providing leadership in many of the apparel categories designed to suit a man's lifestyles. As for tactics, the fashion photography is rather static — reminding us of the typical catalogue (without the informative product descriptions unfortunately). Apart from the barely noticeable vertically placed designer name, information is lacking.

Is appealing and informative copy an anathema to what works in fashion advertising? What is directing the message here? Fashion photography or a strategy? Judging from this use of space, it would appear that if you have to ask about the product or the price, you shouldn't bother shopping here.

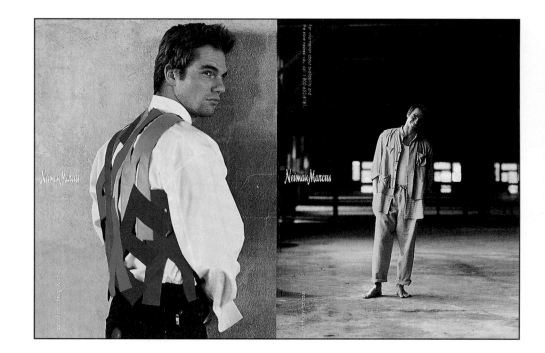

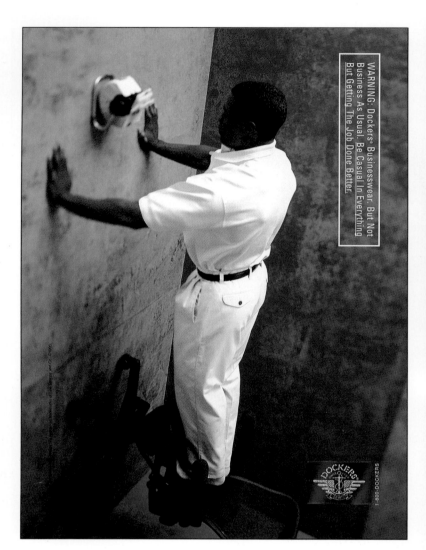

WARNING: Dockers® Businesswear. But Not Business As Usual. Be Casual In Everything But Getting The Job Done Better.

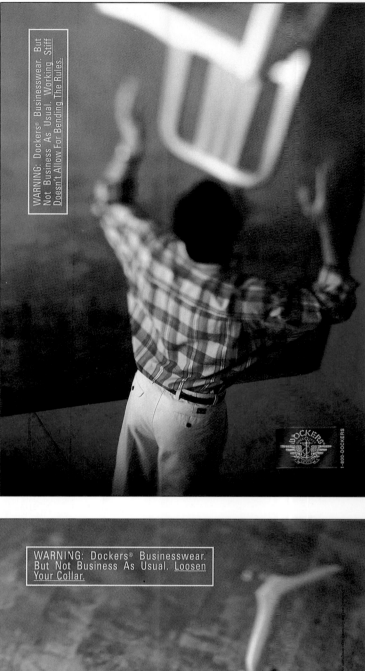

WARNING: Dockers® Businesswear. But Not Business As Usual. Working Stiff Doesn't Allow For Bending The Rules.

WARNING: Dockers® Businesswear. But Not Business As Usual. Loosen Your Collar.

In this campaign Dockers continues to send a lifestyle message to its targeted consumer segments. Their objective is to own a large share of the casual category. The photography and copy reflect that here is a careful study of consumer behavior. The strategy to blend product benefits with consumer benefits is evident in these three ads which portray men who relax and enjoy via the various psychomotor challenges illustrated therein. The creative tactic of putting the copy in a warning block is very effective, inasmuch as it suggests a relationship between Docker's casual Friday Wear and the consumer's total well-being.

Savane's Friday Wear ad focuses more on the product attribute of wrinkle proof — than on a consumer benefit. The headline does make an effective tone statement about the dress code that could help the consumer who agreed with the premise to relate to the brand. The photography is effective in reinforcing the style-appeal as well as the performance promised by the headline and copy. Does the ad also suggest that "when the starch goes out of the dress code" — the feet go up on the conference table? Oh well, we had to show the product to advantage, somehow... ???

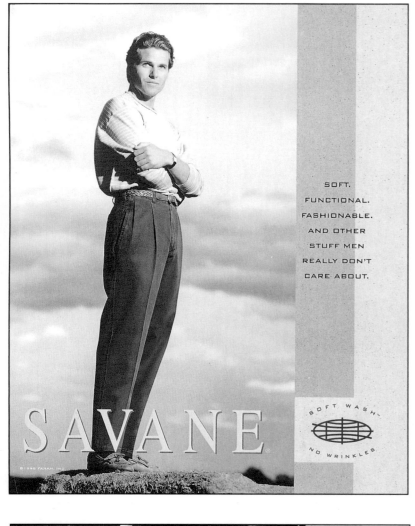

SOFT.
FUNCTIONAL.
FASHIONABLE.
AND OTHER
STUFF MEN
REALLY DON'T
CARE ABOUT.

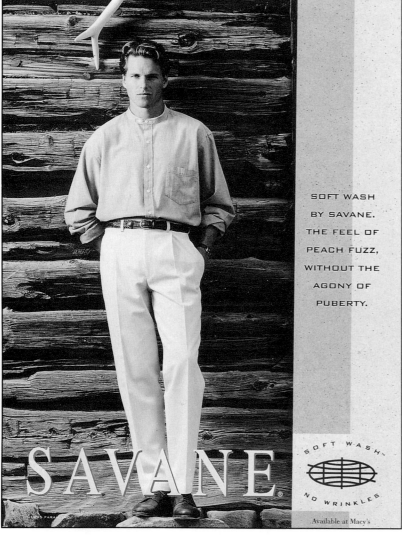

SOFT WASH
BY SAVANE.
THE FEEL OF
PEACH FUZZ,
WITHOUT THE
AGONY OF
PUBERTY.

One of the few new trends in fashion is the recent introduction of wrinkle-free fabrics in men's wear. Savane and Haggar have brought this message to the world of casual comfort clothing. What more could a consumer, wife or mother ask for?

Savane takes a masculine tone and artistic approach to this message. The khaki color scheme along with the outdoor, log cabin backgrounds adds to the total message that is speaking to the male customer, or the female who buys for him. Their graphic logo includes the key benefit —"Soft Wash No Wrinkles".

To attract men of few words, this message gets through quickly and clearly. It delivers product benefits that ideally suit the man whose personal positioning includes looking "neat".

The Haggar campaign is having fun with the stereotyped boy and man who do not know how to coordinate a wardrobe. In the top ad, the audience is the mother who buys her son's clothing. Notice the tone of the copy. It says: "Get him a pair of..." " He'll love it even if it doesn't clash." The teenage "son" in the photograph and the headline are attention getting, the copy delivers the Unique Selling Points of Haggar's "Wrinkle-Free khakis" that are coordinated outfits. Problem-solving with relevant, workable solutions. What more could a teenager ask for? Thanks Mom!

The Haggar logo also incorporates their slogan — "Haggar Stuff you can wear."

The second ad is directed toward a man who needs a wardrobe makeover by a personal shopper. Knowing that he is not likely to seek that kind of help, perhaps Haggar is his answer. This is done in a non-intimidating manner that informs the reader (potential customer) that: "Your mother would be proud. Shocked, but proud." After all, she was the last person who helped him get dressed in the morning — back when he looked acceptable.

Humor can be a marvelous communications tool when used carefully. Haggar has handled it very well.

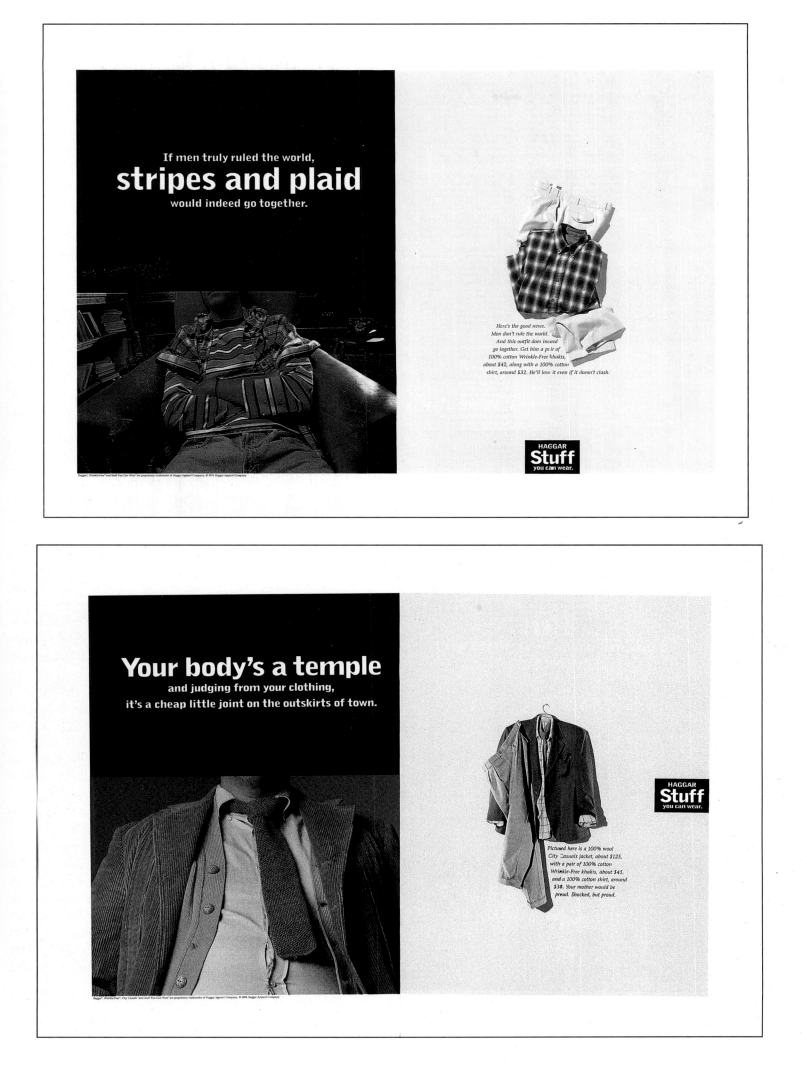

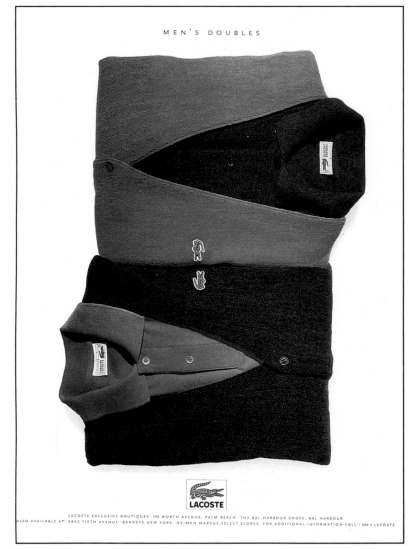

The fashion advertiser's objective is to get consumers to prefer its brand and/or store. Lacoste has been reestablishing itself as "The Authentic. The Original." — after being beaten back by the competition from companies like Ralph Lauren Polo and The Gap.

The two Lacoste ads feature the product without models as fashionable color stores. The "Men's Doubles" ad provides a wardrobe choice with coordinated sweaters. The message is given in a sports context and the Lacoste exclusive boutiques are located in golf resort communities. They chose the right theme for the right target market.

The ad with the stack of multiple color polo shirts is in direct competition with The Gap's ads and folded merchandise store image. The message is three-fold: to establish that Lacoste is the original designer of this style polo/golf shirt; that they have a wide range of colors to choose from or to collect; and that they are made available only in their own exclusive boutiques and select, upscale specialty stores.

Pro golfer **Tom Lehman** avoiding the rough in the Valley of Fire, NV. [Climbing gear from the Dockers Golf. line]

Dockers is one of the great product and advertising successes in fashion history. They started with a strong marketing concept and have followed it through in all aspect of their marketing and communications.

This sports-specific campaign takes Dockers Golfwear to new heights — The headline reflects both the product's range and the consumer's attitude to know no bounds — a winning combination. With pro-golfer Tom Lehman as their model, captured on film in very exotic "beyond golf" environments, Dockers establishes their message visually and then verbally. He is playing golf in rough terrain where the play on words implies multiple-use clothing — "Climbing gear," "Swimwear", and "Survival wear" — from the Dockers Golf line.

Every element of design and copy in this campaign is well conceived and executed: The decision to call the collection "Dockers Golf" could limit them if their strategy did not successfully communicate that the products can go beyond golf alone. Placing the clothes folded over the golf club makes the golf connection, while their pro golfer model maneuvers beyond the green, as featured in photo album form. The logo imprinted on an actual golf ball, placed in the lower right corner of each ad, provides a strong identity to the collection and helps position Dockers as a brand that is now "dedicated" to the golfer.

Pro golfer **Tom Lehman** carrying the pond at Lake Powell, UT. [Swimwear from the Dockers Golf. collection]

Pro golfer **Tom Lehman** getting out of trouble in Death Valley, CA. [Survival wear from the Dockers Golf. line]

WILLIE NELSON/at play

THE ARROW COMPANY
EST 1851

This man's best friend is a horse. And when you own the town, no one's going to tell you that you can't bring your horse inside.

No rhinestone cowboy, Willie is partial to weather-beaten jeans, worn-in boots and a 100% cotton denim Arrow 1851 shirt.

Nothing says "Willie Nelson" like his signature red bandanna, which actually has his name custom-printed right on it.

Welcome to Luck, Texas, Willie's own personal ghost town. "When you're here, you're in luck. When you're not here, you're out of luck."

Mr. Nelson has graciously donated his appearance fee to Farm Aid.

© 1994 Cluett Peabody Co., Inc.

at work/

A

TONY BENNETT/at work

THE ARROW COMPANY
EST 1851

The set list. It's all about finding the right tempos, the right nuances. Sound easy? "It took me ten years to write this list."

"I like it understated, I don't like it obvious." It's a philosophy that's apparent in Tony's clothing as well as his music. Case in point: his classic white Arrow 1851 wrinkle-free dress shirt.

The flowers are a reminder of the great Duke Ellington, who would send a dozen roses whenever he'd written a new song.

The dressing room at Radio City Music Hall is a place Tony is intimately familiar with. No wonder, since he lives only a block away.

Tony Bennett's art isn't limited to singing, as these sketches show. His favorite subjects are other performers. "I always paint from life and 98% of the time I'm around musicians."

Mr. Bennett has graciously donated his appearance fee to the Juvenile Diabetes Foundation.

Available at The Boston Store, P.A. Bergners, and Carson Pirie Scott

© 1994 Cluett Peabody Co., Inc.

at work/at play

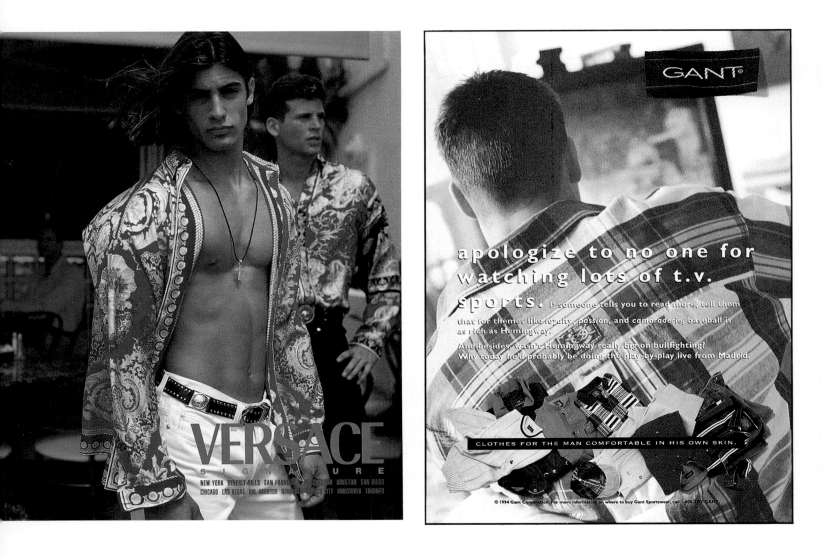

How can we market shirts, let us count the ways...

A company that probably has seen almost as many different advertising campaigns as it has shirt designs, is the longstanding firm of The Arrow Company (since 1851). They have used celebrities in their advertising over the years. Arrow brings their target audience closer to the stars who set fashion trends and style standards.

Representing two very opposite, yet equally appealing styles are Willie Nelson and Tony Bennett. Singers with unforgettable voices and personal styles. Going behind the scenes in their off-stage moments is an entertaining treat for the reader. The celebrities' association with the Arrow Shirt brand adds status to its image.

The selling message that Arrow has shirts for both "at work/at play" is clearly delivered throughout the campaign. The art and copy support this lifestyle message.

An additional public relations message is also given by stating that the models' fees have gone to the charities supported by these celebrities.

On this page we see a good example of two very different male target markets. Do you think they will be found at the same clubs or sporting events? Knowing and profiling the desired target market are crucial to every element of a campaign — from the strategy to the message design, to the photography, to the media placement.

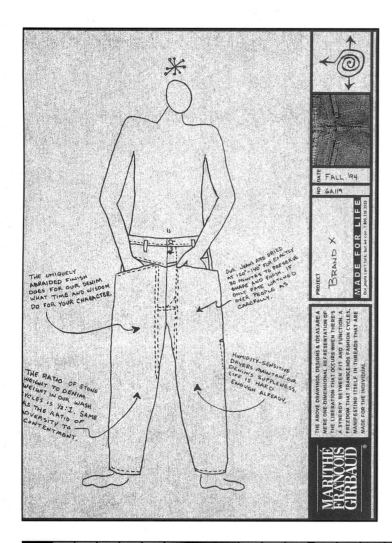

Generation Xers have their own approach to life and living. Remember they didn't get to experience the first round of mini skirts and go-go boots.

Here are three very different attention-getting approaches using photography, computer-composed art with photography, and graphic illustration. To communicate with the post baby-boom generations, advertisers believe they must speak in a visual, MTV-culture language.

The Marithé Francois Girbaud jeans ad is very clever and informative. It delivers both product and lifestyle messages that are relevant to the target market.

Diesel and Gaultier Jean's are using powerful visuals to get the reader's attention and build a unique image for the brand. It would appear this generation is looking for answers to "Successful Living" and "Safe Sex Forever" — but is this in a heaven or hell? There is much to question and much to learn in the advertising of our day.

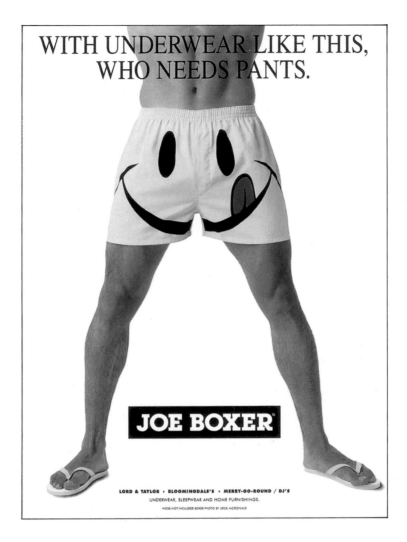

WITH UNDERWEAR LIKE THIS,
WHO NEEDS PANTS.

JOE BOXER

LORD & TAYLOR • BLOOMINGDALE'S • MERRY-GO-ROUND / DJ'S
UNDERWEAR, SLEEPWEAR AND HOME FURNISHINGS.
NOSE-NOT-INCLUDED BOXER PHOTO BY JOCK MCDONALD

WITH UNDERWEAR LIKE THIS,
WHO NEEDS PANTS.

JOE BOXER

DILLARD'S • MARSHALL FIELD'S • THE BROADWAY
UNDERWEAR, SLEEPWEAR AND HOME FURNISHINGS. USA 1-800-992-9406. CANADA 1-800-268-7939.
JOE'S WILD ONE BOXER PHOTO BY JOCK MCDONALD

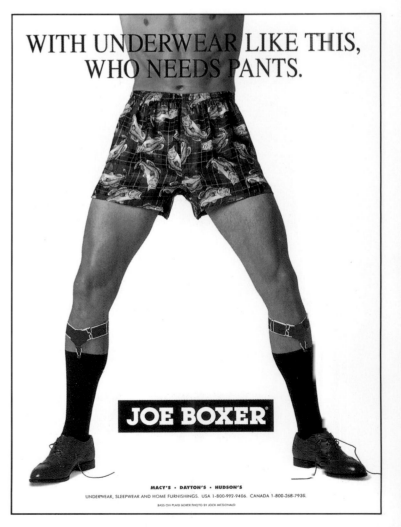

WITH UNDERWEAR LIKE THIS,
WHO NEEDS PANTS.

JOE BOXER

MACY'S • DAYTON'S • HUDSON'S
UNDERWEAR, SLEEPWEAR AND HOME FURNISHINGS. USA 1-800-992-9406. CANADA 1-800-268-7939.
BASS ON PLAID BOXER PHOTO BY JOCK MCDONALD

Who would have ever thought that boxer shorts could become a fashion trend and a collector's item? Will wonders never cease? The Joe Boxer mystique and its brand popularity are a modern day fashion phenomenon.

In these two campaigns, Joe Boxer establishes his brand with relevant humor, "With Underwear Like this, Who Needs Pants." What a great way to gain brand identity and consumer loyalty! Women's lace camisoles came out from under, thanks to companies like Victoria's Secret. Now it's the men's turn — viva la boxer shorts!

And in "Change Daily!" we hear the advice of every careful mother — "What if you're in an accident?" By featuring men who fight fires and cowboys who ride the range, we get the message that these are worn by "Real Men" who ride their underwear hard. Joe Boxer has designed a wide range of shorts to satisfy every type of guy.

The company has also gone into "Underwear Cyberspace". They are on the Internet communicating daily with their customers/fans. Joe Boxer has taken to heart the advice to "have fun with your work".

Fashion Advertising...
"SOFT-SELL" or "HARD-SELL"?

WHAT IS THE SELLING style in fashion advertising? "Soft-sell" or "Hard-sell"? Soft-sell or hard-sell, fashion advertising now has to build the brand character — whether it be a designer name, company label or the store-as-a-brand.

Soft-sell has been the traditional approach of the fashion designer and/or producer. Soft-sell has used the visual rather than copy to speak to the audience. Its long range objectives were not necessarily to request specific consumer behavior such as the retailer's "buy it now from my store".

The strategy has been to convey a message that connects the brand to the consumer's self-image. The tactics were created to reference this through an illustration or photograph of an attractive and appealing fashion model. Meanings in soft-sell fashion advertising included idealizations and promises more than product benefits and comparisons.

Hard-sell used brand and product attributes, consumer benefits, and price to differentiate products and the stores that featured them. Quality, price, and value promises were offered and comparisons made with the competition. There is more copy in hard-sell fashion advertising. The copy provides product information that is needed by the consumer in order to make an immediate decision to purchase.

Today's fashion advertising needs to develop a tone appropriate for a more information-driven society and a more knowledgeable consumer. It must be an appropriate blend of soft-sell and hard-sell. It requires a mix of fantasy and idealization implemented by the esthetic quality of its layout, art, and copy. It should include more information about product and brand differentiation than ever before. It demands a focus on consumer needs, offering more solutions than promises — more product benefits and more value-pricing.

Being on strategy in fashion advertising now requires an approach that is developed through insights into its consumers' values, attitudes, and lifestyles. Fashion advertising should create themes that provide its target segment consumers with a real reason to prefer the brand, and to shop the store. Fashion advertising in the past relied largely on emotional appeals aimed at the heart of the consumer. In today's more competitive marketplace, the fashion advertiser needs to add rational appeals aimed at the mind of the consumer.

WHAT WORKS IN

Children's

FASHION
ADVERTISING

Paint and ketchup and glue and mud and juice and markers and chalk and ravioli. Now that's what little girls are made of.

Sugar and spice and everything nice?!?!? We don't think so. These days, little girls get into just about anything (Isn't it great?) Which is why here at Healthtex, we suggest you get your child into something that's easy to wash. Like the outfit shown here. Or the dozens of other really cute new styles we have this spring. Just call us at 1-800-554-7637 to find out more. As for snakes, snails and puppy dog tails, no problem. All of our boys' clothes are just as easy to wash. 1-800-554-7637

Healthtex

Questions? Call 1-800-554-7637. Look for Healthtex at The Bon Marché, Boscov's and Lazarus.

Remember; zippers are like boogie men. If you get too close, they bite.

Elastic waistbands are a lot easier for kids and busy parents to handle than zippers. Not to mention, they don't pinch your skin. (Ouch!) And when you put them in our cool-looking clothes, you have it made. Call us to find out more. Like our clothes, our operators are very friendly.

Healthtex

1-800-554-7637

Questions? Call 1-800-554-7637. Look for Healthtex at JCPenney.

Here are Beth, Ellen and Jimmy showing off their new clothes. (Ellen and Jimmy are imaginary friends. Just play along.)

Aren't they cute? Especially Beth in her plaid flannel jumper and matching turtleneck. Call toll-free to find out more about our fall playwear, like colorful denims and fun coveralls. We'll gladly give you some fashion tips for your child and her, er, friends.

Healthtex

1-800-554-7637

Questions? Call 1-800-554-7637. Look for Healthtex at Kids 'R' Us.

He has his mother's eyes, grandma's nose and sweats like his dad.

Attention-getting visuals and the cutest kids in town dominate the campaign. Headlines speak in everyday language and feature the product line for children in broad terms with emphasis on specific features that set the Healthtex line apart. There is a tonality of ease and comfort and everyday living with a charm that makes each ad not just readable but lovable beyond the dynamics of the specific message. One senses an understanding the advertiser has of the reader with a charm and involvement in both visual and copy. The more you read the more you want to read. The more you know, the more you want to get to know. Healthtex, good for kids and healthy for your psyche.

Introducing sweats kids can call their own. Playwear Sweats from Healthtex.

There you are in the mall with your child. You bump into a friend you haven't seen in a while. She goes ga-ga, pinching your child's cheek and tousling his hair. "He looks just like his dad," she says. You proudly nod. Then you realize she's referring to those old, gray sweats he's wearing.

At Healthtex, we're as tired of boring traditional sweats as you are. That's why we designed our new Playwear Sweats to be as cute as your kid. (Well, almost.) Our sweats look just as good sitting in preschool as rolling around in the yard. All our outfits come in fashionable, fun colors that your kid will love.

Apricot, peacock, spruce...just about any color you can think of. And they come in all sorts of exciting prints, too.

Hold on, there's more. You'll also find a playful assortment of appliqués, wonderful embroidery details and sports patches. Not to mention little ruffled tops and layered leg pants. Best of all, you can mix and match the tops and bottoms to create all sorts of fresh, new outfits.

But don't worry. Our Playwear Sweats are much more than pretty clothes. They're constructed to survive all of the running, jumping, hopping, sliding, skipping, falling, climbing and crawling your kid

can dish out. (Not to mention rolling.)

And we didn't sacrifice one thread of comfort. Our fleece is cut from an easy-care, high-cotton blend so it breathes. And our sweats are sized generously, so they're easy to pull on and off. In other words, they're kind of like soft, roomy suits of armor.

To find out more, just give us a call at 1-800-554-7637. We'll answer any questions you have.

Now go on and throw out those old, gray sweats. On second thought, keep yours, Dad. You might look a little ridiculous in one of our puffed posy print outfits. 1-800-554-7637

Healthtex

A VF COMPANY. A LEADER IN QUALITY APPAREL. ©1994 Healthtex, Inc.

Call us toll-free at 1-800-554-7637 for the store nearest you, or if you simply have questions.

IT CAME from the YARD

OUT OF THE **MUD** IT ROSE...

TO TRACK ITS **SOILED** SNEAKERS HOME TO MOM.

Eaaaahhhh! Once a darling, clean and well-groomed child, now a barely identifiable blob of mud. Ah, cruel fate! Of course, since both the kid and the sneakers can be washed it's not really all that bad. Yes, Keds® TrueWash® leather sneakers are machine washable and dryable. That means they won't shrink or crack. In fact, they've been thoroughly tested by some relatively sane scientists and, even after numerous washings, the colors stay bright, the leathers stay soft and supple and the stitching stays intact! And, as if that weren't enough excitement, Keds sneakers are available in infants, toddlers, girls and boys styles. Take a piece of motherly advice. Outfit your little mud-worshippers in a pair of washable, dryable leather Keds sneakers before they venture outside! Because the mud from which they come today is the same mud they'll find their way back to tomorrow!

© 1994 Keds Corporation

TRUE WASH® *Washable*/**DRYABLE** | **Keds** | **THEY** *FEEL* **GOOD**™

IT THRASHES IT KICKS IT FLAILS AT ITS PREY

TALES FROM THE CRIB

Who AMONG US WOULD DARE PUT ITS SNEAKERS ON?

The mere thought paralyzes most parents with fear . . . putting their toddler's sneakers on! Take heart! Our product designers have boisterous kids, too. That's why they created new Keds® Easy-Sneaks™. Keds Easy-Sneaks look just like the regular sneakers you know and love, but they go on without the all-too-familiar struggle. How is it humanly possible? Well, Keds Easy-Sneaks have easy on and off features like a patent-pending "easy-fit" hourglass tongue that stays open when it's pulled open, stretch laces that cinch closed, or easy-to-pull straps that simply do away with laces altogether. And, adults and children alike are hypnotically entranced by the many boys and girls styles. Look for Keds Easy-Sneaks in a store near you! Because kids can be monsters, the least we could do is create sneakers to go on them.

© 1994 Keds Corporation

EASY-SNEAKS™ *Easy* ON *And* OFF | **Keds** | **THEY** *FEEL* **GOOD**™

Active children are the visual focus of the campaigns. Durability of product line is accentuated, highlighting the stylish, yet rugged flexibility of the garments in a playful environment. Playful, but serious that is. In all cases, the advertiser provides specific performance assurances while style and value are the solid underpinnings. Tonality is warm, comfortable and inviting, and encourages the reader's involvement. These ads are faithful to each brand's strategy, yet each is quite distinctive from the other. Keds and Levi's have their own unique look, yet each offers similar product benefits… style, durability and value. What more can any parent want for their kids?

For the time-starved parent, the message must be delivered quickly. Keds uses the old B-movie poster format to attract attention and interest; then build desire with the solution to their daily horrors; and their slogan helps the reader take action to buy Keds for their kids — because "THEY FEEL GOOD."

Levi's device for a quick read is to use large, bold type that states its own message. This works well for the reader who doesn't have time for more: "A guarantee so strong nobody ever gets soaked. Little Levi's."

esprit de corps gymnasts, mill valley california

ESPRIT

Great color photos of active kids highlight each campaign. While emphasis is placed on style or product feature, copy is presented in a somewhat tongue-in-cheek vernacular. "What to wear for long talks with a friend," features a child listening to her dog. "Every baby needs proper support behind the neck," refers to your support while holding the baby rather than from a specific feature inherent in the product. Headlines are all attention-getting and arresting and together with big visuals, they literally force the readers' involvement. Tone is light and playful yet factual and definitive in terms of consumer benefit. Each ad takes its own tack in presentation, yet there is much similarity between campaigns and therefore easy to confuse one campaign with another ... a no-no according to the research gurus.

Lumber Jack thermal top & fleece overall

What To Wear For
Long Talks With A Friend

Moms say that our clothes last for decades. They say that their kids love them. They say that they're comfortable, stylish and made with traditional quality. We don't know, however, what dogs have to say.

Carter's

If they could just stay little 'til their Carter's wear out."

Every baby
needs proper support
behind the neck.

It is wonderful to hold your baby in your arms and of course it is essential to do so correctly. Equally important is having the right clothes to dress your child in.

At Ladybird we've been specialising in these clothes for years. Our fabrics are carefully selected for their softness, to ensure they won't irritate a baby's skin.

The dyes are tested rigorously. They mustn't come out in the wash. Or more importantly, in a baby's mouth.

We scrutinise every popper. Every button. We even test the seams to be sure they can withstand the antics of the most boisterous babe.

High standards admittedly. Standards, we're proud to say, that often exceed the legal requirements.

Take our babysuits. We've made sure the feet are a little larger so your baby can wear socks for extra warmth.

Indeed if you do take one of our babysuits and find it isn't quite right, don't worry. As with all our clothes, it's covered by our customer satisfaction guarantee. (Simply bring the item back and we'll happily exchange it for something that is right, or we'll refund your money in full.)

After all, Ladybird clothes aren't just made with babies in mind. They're designed to be a support to you too.

WOOLWORTHS

Looking for clothes that mix 'n' match?

If you want clothes that go together, you just need to know where to look: OshKosh B'Gosh. We offer coordinated combinations, and quality, to boot.

OSH KOSH B'gosh
THE GENUINE ARTICLE

Kids' clothes where everything goes.

Some things were just meant to go together.

Kids and OshKosh B'Gosh clothes have always been inseparable. But the fact that all our separates go together is what really makes them stand apart.

OSH KOSH B'gosh
THE GENUINE ARTICLE

Kids' clothes where everything goes.

A picture is worth a thousand words. Or two thousand as the case may be. In this case the pictures tell the whole story in a warm and compelling manner. The Esprit campaign for Nordstrom features kids, dogs and clothes, and they're all friends. And all are comfortable in their environment as they are with each other. In the ad featuring the brown knapsack, the young girl in her outfit is presented as one look and the Esprit knapsack adds just the right fashion finish. It's "what's important".

WHAT WORKS IN

Accessories

FASHION
ADVERTISING

Elegance, quality and high style are expressed by visual metaphors in these ads. The lack of copy assumes that there is a high level of consumer awareness and distinctive understanding of the merchandise. The comparison is between Chanel's use of reality and vivid colors, and Bulgari's distinctive creative expression in soft pastels. Each attempts to set a truly unique tone. In both cases the message reflects the highest in quality and the top of the mark.

Dior, DeBeers and Tiffany. Visually compelling in terms of quality and image. Fashion photography skillfully used to focus on a dramatic presentation of merchandise is the strategy in these ads.

Full page, full bleed, and full of warmth and excitement, the campaigns have a singular objective in product presentation and in elegant form. It all says top quality and top of the line by the most careful reproduction of facet, stone-setting and precious metallurgy. The Tiffany metaphors — "bone cuff" and "snake necklace" create a tone that helps the customer "feel" the jewelry.

The DeBeers campaign creates an experience that makes a fabulous promise to the wearer. Tiffany's "fringe necklace" ad reflects a positioning strategy calculated to reinforce their image by presenting "masterworks" of jewelry design. The Dior ad is typical of fashion advertising that relies on the designer brand to carry the message. In this case the merchandise suggests a coordinated ensemble for emphatic adornment of the ears, wrist and neck.

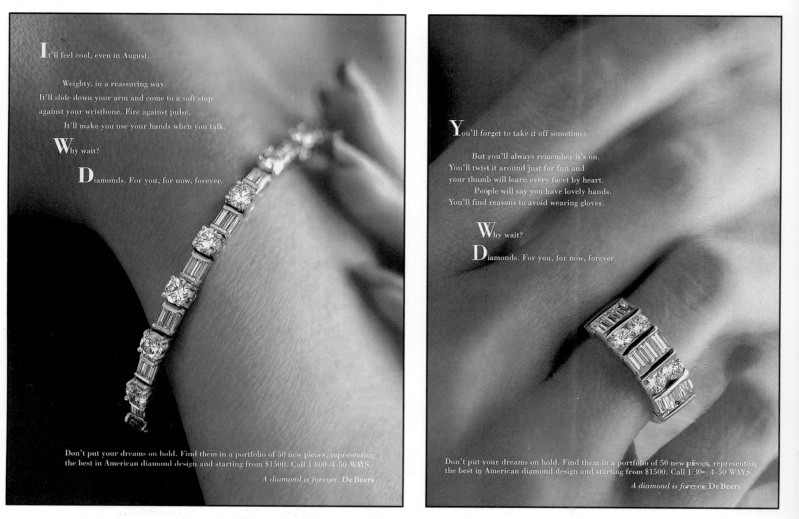

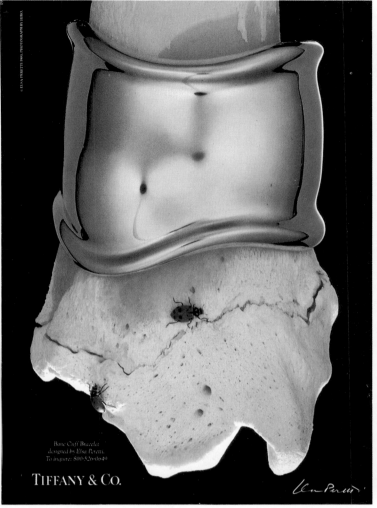

*Bone Cuff Bracelet
designed by Elsa Peretti.
To inquire: 800-526-0649*

TIFFANY & CO.

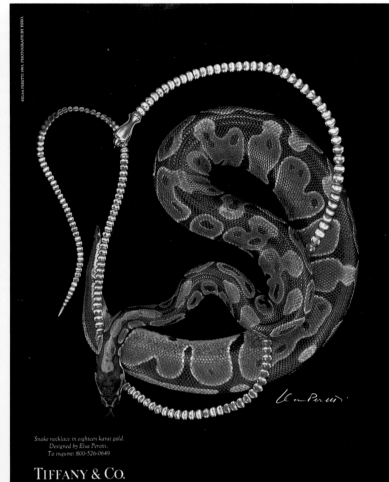

*Snake necklace in eighteen karat gold.
Designed by Elsa Peretti.
To inquire: 800-526-0649*

TIFFANY & CO.

JEAN SCHLUMBERGER, ARTIST

The moment Mme. Schiaparelli
discovered him in Paris,
the furor began.
A genius breaking all the rules.
Soon he was at Tiffany,
creating masterworks for a
small circle of elegant women
and museum curators
worldwide.

The Fringe Necklace in eighteen karat gold with diamonds, $39,250.

TIFFANY & CO.

NEW YORK ATLANTA BAL HARBOUR BEVERLY HILLS BOSTON CHICAGO DALLAS HONOLULU HOUSTON PALM BEACH PHILADELPHIA SAN DIEGO
SAN FRANCISCO SOUTH COAST PLAZA TORONTO TROY WASHINGTON, D.C. TO INQUIRE: 800-526-0649

Available at Neiman Marcus selected stores only. To receive a free brochure, please write Trisha, Bally, One Bally Place, New Rochelle, NY 10801

BALLY®

The Bally campaign fantasizes how one's feet enjoy the experience of their shoes. The consumer benefits implied are ultimate pleasure and virtual euphoria. Bally's technique is highly graphic with barely a touch of copy... the visual image conveys the story. It is not possible to confuse the individualized style of this campaign with any other footwear, accessory, and apparel company. They are truly feet apart.

The ads on page 80 each feature one shoe style — appropriate footwear for this fantasy. The layout is consistent in bringing the actual "product in the tissued box" to the customer's eye.

The ads featured above are more institutional with no products shown. They continue to build brand-name awareness for all of Bally's products. The foot print is the visual metaphor for the original Bally product — footwear made of the finest Italian leather.

Felicia de Chabris collects clocks
from the '50s and beyond.
Aside from the practical aspects
(like never being late for
an appointment), they take her
back to an era when things
weren't so rushed. Which brings
us to her Cole-Haan shoes.
They, too, stand the test of time.
Just a little less conspicuously.

COLE·HAAN

From an inspired collection of footwear, The Women's Halena in bone, platinum or silver nappa
For information write: Cole-Haan, Department P2, One Cole-Haan Drive, Yarmouth, Maine 04096.

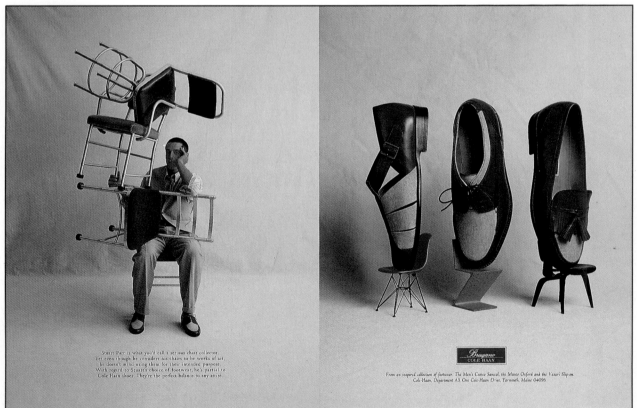

Stuart Parr is what you'd call a serious chair collector.
Yet even though he considers his chairs to be works of art,
he doesn't mind using them for their intended purpose.
With regard to Stuart's choice of footwear, he's partial to
Cole-Haan shoes. They're the perfect balance to any attire.

Bragano
COLE·HAAN

From an inspired collection of footwear, The Men's Cuneo Sandal, the Museo Oxford and the Vasari Slip-on.
Cole-Haan, Department A3, One Cole-Haan Drive, Yarmouth, Maine 04096.

How many pairs of shoes are enough? Well, if they are a collectible element of fashion as presented by Cole Haan, the answer can be found inside your closet. The versatility of one's wardrobe is measured by the extent of one's footwear collection.

Cole Haan presents footwear in as diversified a manner as fashion, and as the finishing touch in the completion of any wardrobe. In all ads, the product is the dominant focal element surrounded by materials which enhance diversity of use, day or night, casual or formal. But, who will foot the bill?

This is Claudio Gottardo's globe collection.
He likes to see how different globe makers
interpret the world. Different sizes, different
colors, different materials. (At least they
all agree on shape.) As for Cole-Haan shoes?
Claudio appreciates that they're
just as functional on land as they are on
the other two-thirds of the earth.

COLE·HAAN
SPORTING

From an inspired collection of footwear. The Men's Pennant Boat Moccasin in an array of colors. Crafted in Maine, USA.
Cole-Haan, Department A2, One Cole-Haan Drive, Yarmouth, Maine 04096.

Tracy Smith collects classic telephones.
Not only does she believe in the art of
conversation, she thinks it's important
to express oneself in an interesting way.
Which may be why she's attracted to
Cole-Haan shoes. They tend to make
a point. In a most articulate fashion.

COLE·HAAN

From an inspired collection of footwear. The Women's Zerto Sandal and Zadie Thong.
Cole-Haan, Department R2, One Cole-Haan Drive, Yarmouth, Maine 04096.

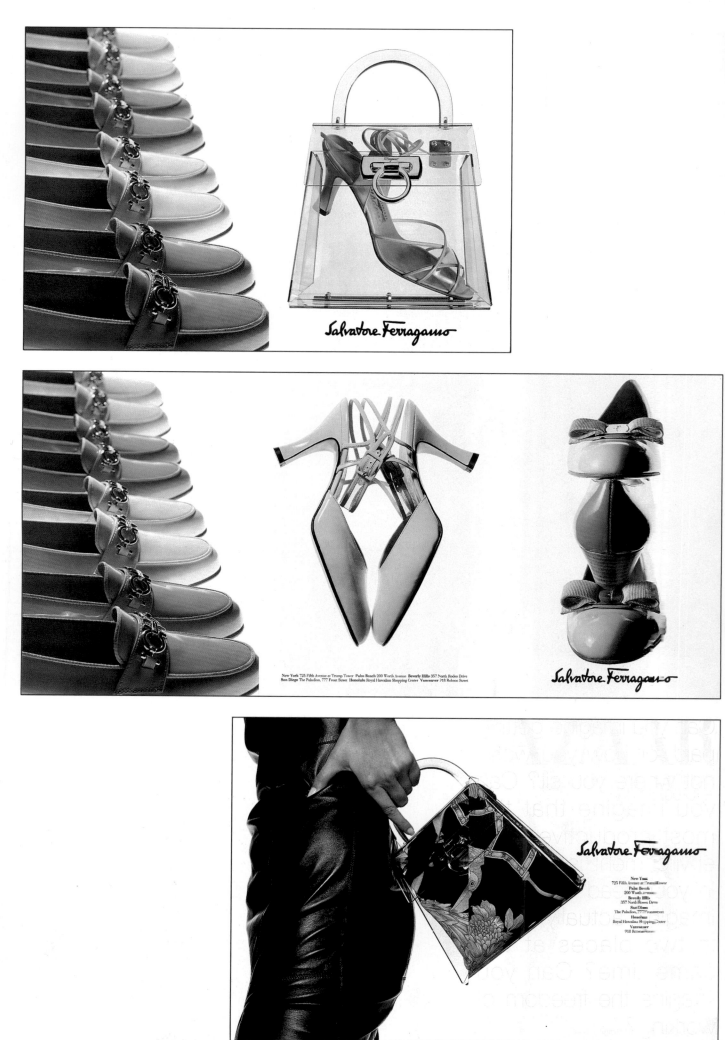

charles david
by Nathalie M

Charles David, Beverly Center

charles david
by Nathalie M

Ferragamo's emphasis is on the attributes of the product… Charles David's ads dramatize the experience of wearing the product and tell a color story. Ferragamo displays product so that the consumer can "examine" the materials and construction in each ad. Layout designs are distinctive and unique and utilize a good balance between merchandise to white space. The Charles David ads reflect the move to "nostalgia and *déjà vu* marketing" in its "girl on a swing" and "september morn" looks. (We're not so sure how traditional is the "legs akimbo" crouch — but it does show what the product can do.) Very different strategies in advertising, between the two. Style and elegance in both approaches.

charles david
by Nathalie M

Charles David Stores

FOR STORE LOCATIONS OR MORE INFORMATION CALL 1-800-388-6785

FOR STORE LOCATIONS OR MORE INFORMATION CALL 1-800-388-6785

For the Louis Vuitton Cup our famous canvas goes nautical.

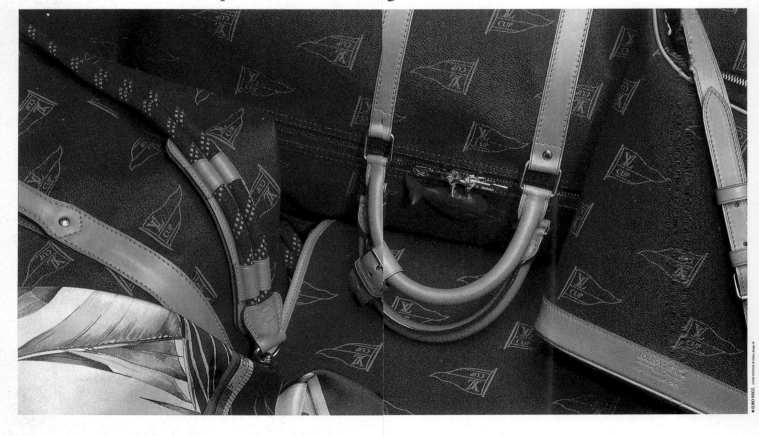

Available for a limited time in select Louis Vuitton shops. For more information, please call 1 800 458 7962.

The Louis Vuitton Cup. Challenger races for the America's Cup. January–April 1995. International teams race for the opportunity to challenge The United States on the high seas of San Diego. In celebration, Louis Vuitton's famous Monogram canvas goes nautical with a numbered limited edition collection.

Louis Vuitton

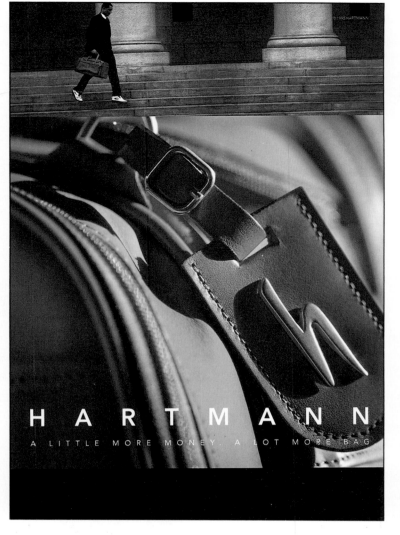

Not the same old bag to be sure, the issue of distinction in these three is the bag itself, presented in each ad to make them the central message. In each case, style and elegance are always emphasized. Elegance is the basic underpinning. These single item ads obviously are intended not only to sell the advertised product, but to create a positioning of brand image for the company. Each contains a distinctly different strategy.

The Hartmann and especially the Louis Vuitton ads show the products in a setting suggesting the consumer's experience with them. They articulate product benefits (even if it costs "a little more money"). The Gucci ads are typical Gucci — inasmuch as they rely solely on the logo to suggest value.

Louis Vuitton luggage: always the unexpected, since 1854.

Louis Vuitton bags: always the un expected, since 1854.

Louis Vuitton bags: always the un expected, since 1854.

The travel motif permeates the campaign for Louis Vuitton bags and luggage. For anyone who travels, it is not hard to comprehend its relevance. It does reiterate and support the unexpected pleasures and surprises one comes upon while adventuring abroad. It is apparent that awareness is high among the target audience and essentially this is used as reminder advertising. It is expected that the name alone will connote a certain attitude toward the product and each specific item in each ad presents its own arresting visuals. Great color, excellent use of white space and a distinctive tonality unlike any other travel bag.

In today's world of clutter and information overload, advertisers must find a way to stand out from the crowd. Louis Vuitton cannot be mistaken with any other company. They are positioning themselves as a catalyst to exciting adventures — providing "always the unexpected". Their bags are no doubt always ready for the unexpected too. They also sell trust in their know-how — "since 1854" tells the reader that they have evolved successfully through every mode of travel.

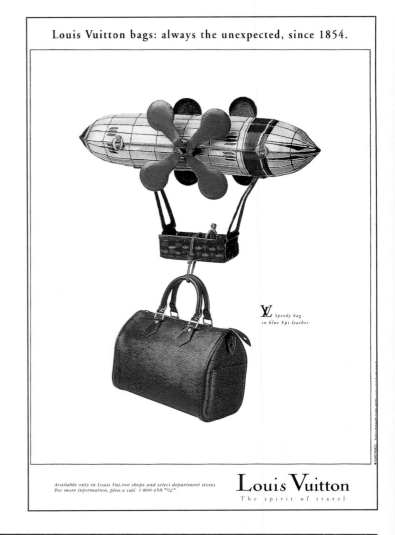

Louis Vuitton bags: always the unexpected, since 1854.

Speedy bag in blue Epi leather.

Available only in Louis Vuitton shops and select department stores. For more information, please call 1-800-458-"92".

Louis Vuitton
The spirit of travel

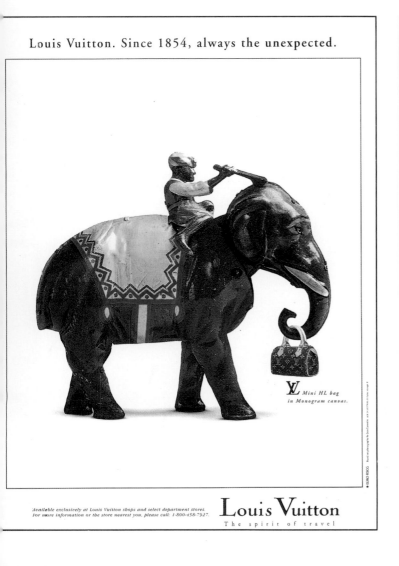

Louis Vuitton. Since 1854, always the unexpected.

Mini HL bag in Monogram canvas.

Available exclusively at Louis Vuitton shops and select department stores. For more information or the store nearest you, please call: 1-800-458-7927.

Louis Vuitton
The spirit of travel

Louis Vuitton. Since 1854, always the unexpected.

Cluny bag in red Epi leather.

Available exclusively at Louis Vuitton shops and select department stores. For more information or the store nearest you, please call: 1-800-458-4133.

Louis Vuitton
The spirit of travel

DOONEY & BOURKE

The All-Weather Leather® Collection is available at 759 Madison Avenue, New York (between 65th and 66th) 212-439-1657, and at Trump Tower, 725 Fifth Avenue, New York 212-308-0520. For a catalog, call 800-546-0398

Judith Leiber
Handbags / Accessories

Bergdorf Goodman   Neiman Marcus   Saks Fifth Avenue

WHAT IS WHIMSICAL?
Singing in the rain, surprise presents,
AND THE NEW BANTAM BAG FROM COACH.

COACH

Introducing the Coach Bantam Bag with convertible straps that, on a whim, can turn a mini backpack into a handbag. Available in a bouquet of new colors such as Coral, Chambray, Pear and Banana, as well as an array of classic Coach colors. Bantam Bag, No. 4152, $220.

TO ORDER, OR FOR A COMPLIMENTARY CATALOGUE, PLEASE CALL 800 262-2411. ALSO AVAILABLE AT COACH STORES, SELECTED DEPARTMENT AND SPECIALTY STORES.

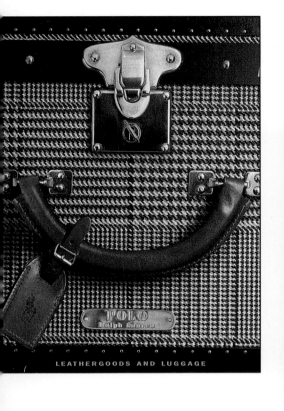

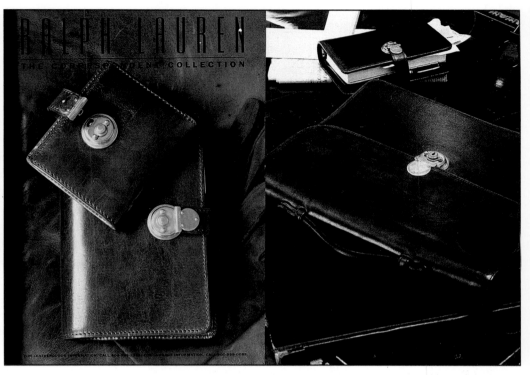

Leather bags, a winner one and all. Whomever the designer, the caliber of elegance bespeaks each style so that one could easily opt to buy them all. Perhaps not readily affordable, the tone clearly says quality and the look is distinctive from others. The one constant … all are at the top of their line. And, each presents product in a delicious surrounding that not only supports product but adds to the value by virtue of image enhancement. The benefits are clear. One simply need to appreciate the status appeal to see it.

In the case of Ralph Lauren's leathergoods and luggage, the close-up photography provides a more tactile feel. The product is touchable, desirable, and within the consumer's reach.

The ads on page 90 send a message about variety of styles and colors. The ads on this page feature coordinated sets. All present strong brand name impact with consistent logo and ad design.

Hermès provides accessories for the colorful customer. From scarves to ties to unique watches, the colorful combinations and contrasts in color dominate the space. Today's customer has a vast array of contrasts to deal with in the world. Hermès can help the customer find what will no doubt distinguish his or her "look".

Each company needs to develop its own U.S.P. (unique selling proposition) that will differentiate it from the competition. When this is established as *the* company known for this characteristic, it's said that the company "owns" that U.S.P. For example, Volvo = safety; Hermès = exquisite fabrics.

The vivid display of colorful merchandise on a black background not only makes the product pop off the page, it also establishes the Hermès look. They have a traditional logo appearing in each ad to establish their heritage within this business. It provides continuity through their campaign as it also appears on the brown imprinted ribbon tieing the products and the consumer's package together.

*Bushels of tomatoes,
lettuce, pumpkins and
escargots abound on
the many ties in the new
Hermès collection.*

21 Highland Park Village
(214) 528-0197

HERMÈS IN THE GARDEN.

HERMÈS
PARIS

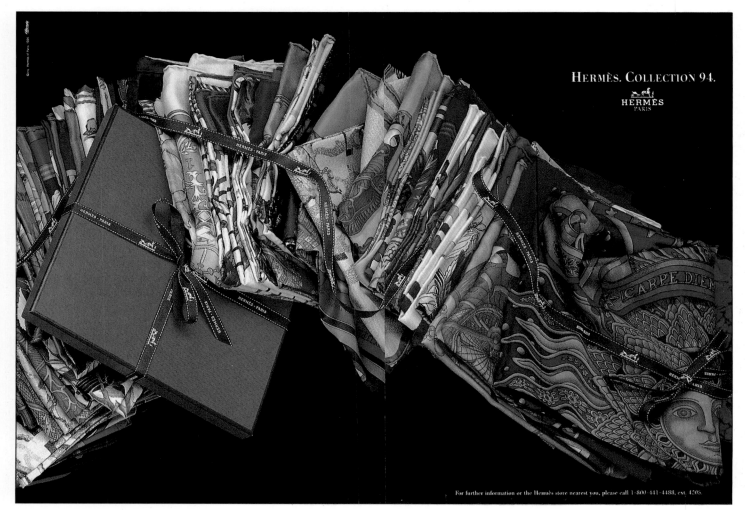

HERMÈS. COLLECTION 94.

HERMÈS
PARIS

For further information or the Hermès store nearest you, please call 1-800-441-4488, ext. 4205.

NEW TECH

Technology is nothing new to Ray-Ban sunglasses. In fact, the brand was developed in the 1930's based on the innovative design and engineering of flying glasses for American pilots. Today's Ray-Ban advanced technology lenses provide optimum choices to meet the needs of a variety of active, outdoor-oriented lifestyles. Advanced technology lenses maintain the Ray-Ban tradition of quality, craftsmanship and protection for those dedicated to light outdoors at the speed of life.

THE WORLD'S MOST ADVANCED DRIVING SUNGLASSES

The Ray-Ban Driving Series Lenses with ChroMax™ Color Contrast Technology are formulated with rare earth elements to selectively filter light from the driving environment so that the reds, greens and ambers of traffic signals, road signs and brake lights appear brighter and are easier to see. An anti-reflective coating on the back of the lens minimizes glare, reducing eye strain and fatigue. Every other sunglass pales by comparison.

10 KARAT GLASS

The Ray-Ban DiamondHard™ Scratch-Protection System is a lens surfacing technology permanently bonded to Ray-Ban lenses. It makes lenses 10X more scratch-resistant than ordinary glass, reduces surface friction for water repellence and provides maximum scratch protection for active, outdoor use. That's why Ray-Ban sunglasses with DiamondHard are called "outrageous."

CATCH AND RELEASE

Ray-Ban Glass Polarized sunglasses "catch" the intense reflections that water and other smooth surfaces bounce into your eyes. A special lens filter traps the polarized reflections, virtually eliminating glare and blind spots. What they "release" is natural color rendition and distortion-free vision. Now you'll have one less excuse when the big one gets away.

NATURAL VISION

The Ray-Ban G-15® gray lens is the best general purpose lens available today and it is only from the makers of Ray-Ban sunglasses. This glass lens is the classic Ray-Ban lens that provides natural color rendition distortion-free vision and optical quality. It is now available in the G-15 XLT lens, which means extra light weight for extra comfort. Recommended for use at least once a day.

THE WORLD'S FINEST SUNGLASSES

GIORGIO ARMANI

OCCHIALI

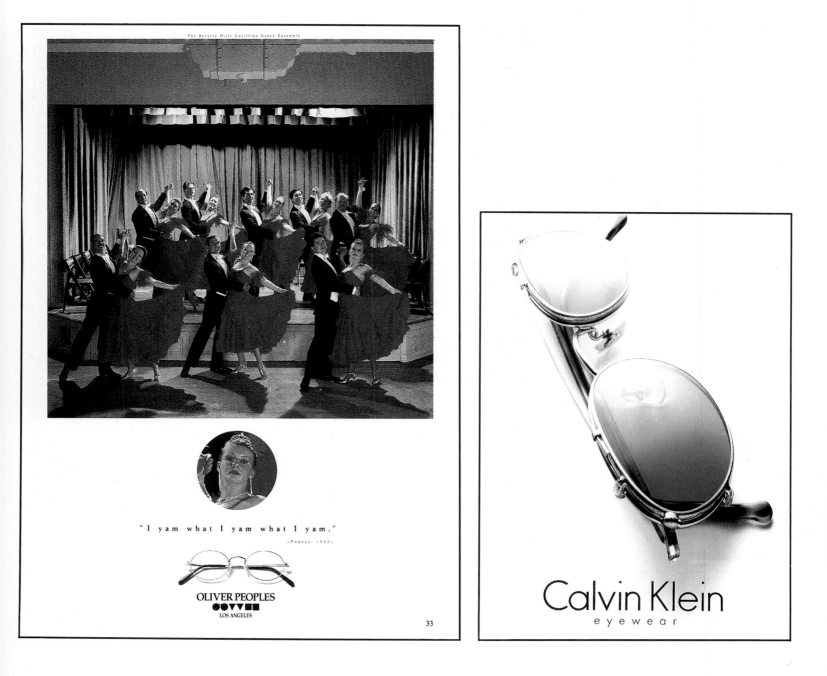

The contrast between "info-sell" and "image-sell" is crystal clear in the "Ray-Ban's new tech" information approach and the Armani, Calvin Klein, Oliver Peoples image approach. Ray-Ban's strategy is designed to appeal to the consumer segment that needs to know how the glasses work. They are selling product attributes and benefits.

Color your glasses beautiful is a strategy used by the eyewear designer to idealize the consumer. The designers, in using different techniques to differentiate product, all come full circle in their presentations which focus on fashion. However one chooses to strategize, today's eyewear is an element of fashion which fits within the consumer's overall fashion consciousness. And fashion is how consumers justify their wardrobe of glasses. Like shoes, each wardrobe contains a broad variety. Different tactics are used, however, Calvin Klein is model-less, while Armani and Ray-Ban are model-plus. Oliver Peoples is L.A. L.A. for sure.

POLO RALPH LAUREN
THE STAINLESS STEEL EYEWEAR COLLECTION

FOR INFORMATION AND STORE LOCATIONS 1-800-560-163E

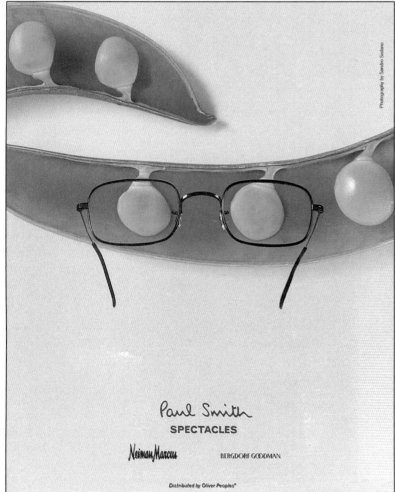

Photography by Sandro Sodano

Paul Smith
SPECTACLES

Neiman Marcus   BERGDORF GOODMAN

Distributed by Oliver Peoples®

It would appear that these eyewear companies have chosen the KISS method of communication—KEEP IT SHORT & SIMPLE!

Polo Ralph Lauren's name is enough to command attention. His new product attribute for eyewear—stainless steel—is presented in the eye exam style: in and out of focus.

Paul Smith's message is unclear and offers no information to explain the "like two peas in a pod" visual reference. What is the message about the product or spectacles collection?

Watches are also an important investment, but they mean less to your health and good looks than do glasses. They signify more about your attitude about time, and how you want to position your own "look." The investment prices of these watches require some serious information to justify the cost.

Both Bulgari and Seiko have automatic and kinetic movements respectively. Seiko's message has more product information and brings the watch up close for a very compelling style appeal. Bulgari uses short copy and a simple visual metaphor. It illustrates a pipeline to demonstrate the watch's main attributes of stainless steel and water resistance.

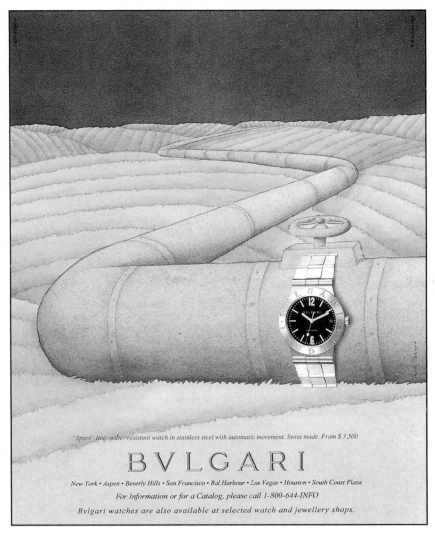

"Sport" line: water resistant watch in stainless steel with automatic movement. Swiss made. From $3,500

BVLGARI

New York • Aspen • Beverly Hills • San Francisco • Bal Harbour • Las Vegas • Houston • South Coast Plaza

For Information or for a Catalog, please call 1-800-644-INFO

Bvlgari watches are also available at selected watch and jewellery shops.

HOW COULD

WE FIT

50
PATENTS
INSIDE?

WE TOOK

OUT THE
BATTERY.

25 years ago, Seiko engineers perfected the quartz watch. Now, they've perfected the quartz watch that never needs a battery. Seiko Kinetic. How amazing is this watch? You supply the power to run it just by the movement of your wrist. (No wonder the people who issue patents know us so well.) Seiko Kinetic. It's not a watch. It's a conversation piece.

Available at these Seiko Authorized Dealers: Reeds Jewelers, Ross Jewelers, Long's Jewelers, Masseys Jewelers and Smart Jewelers.

SEIKO
KINETIC®
Someday all watches will be made this way.

"... I've risked my life to use your Indiglo watch. After my sisters go to sleep I use its light to read their diaries under my blankets" — Marsha Kelly, St. Louis, Mo.

Indiglo by Timex

"While scuba diving for lobsters one night, my wife used her Indiglo watch instead of our flashlight. It was beautiful - they were mesmerized by the soft blue light. So we grabbed them, boiled them and ate them" — Kurt Winselmann, Dania, Fl.

Indiglo by Timex

Watch yourself. You could find that you're running out of time. Not to worry, there's a new Indiglo by Timex for you. Wet or dry, low or high, dark or light, the time is now to get with today's times. Distinctive presentation of product, Timex has a vast array of product for every need and want. Fashionable and forward thinking, reliable and reasonable, Timex time is differentiated by a product benefit that builds the brand.

Readers of both these campaigns can identify with the "voices" that speak to them in these ads. The tone is intimate and humorous. The product is presented as a problem-solver with a bright personality designed to create brand character.

GOOD LOOKING. RELIABLE. BRIGHT.

(IF ONLY THERE WERE MORE MEN LIKE THAT.)

It's everything a woman could ask for. It's handsome. It's got an Indiglo night-light. And unlike what's his name, it'll never let **INDIGLO** you down. To order or for retailers call 1-800-367-8463. BY TIMEX

TIMEX®. IT TAKES A LICKING AND KEEPS ON TICKING®.
©1994 Timex Corp. Indiglo is a registered trademark of Indiglo Corp.

NOW YOU CAN TELL YOUR HUSBAND PRECISELY

WHEN HE STARTED SNORING LAST NIGHT.

Was it 3:00? Was it 5:00? Or was it both? With our Indiglo night-light a push of the button tells you precisely what insane hour it really is. It's also beautiful to stare at **INDIGLO** in the middle of the night. To order or for retailers call 1-800-367-8463. BY TIMEX

TIMEX®. IT TAKES A LICKING AND KEEPS ON TICKING®.
©1994 Timex Corp. Indiglo is a registered trademark of Indiglo Corp.

YOU MAY BE TOO OLD FOR A BLANKIE,

BUT YOU CAN STILL HAVE A NIGHT-LIGHT.

Sure, this watch is rugged and manly. But, then again, with its handy Indiglo night-light it's also the perfect complement to your favorite jammies. There's even a compass **INDIGLO** so you'll never get lost. To order or for retailers call 1-800-367-8463. BY TIMEX

TIMEX®. IT TAKES A LICKING AND KEEPS ON TICKING®.
©1994 Timex Corp. Indiglo is a registered trademark of Indiglo Corp.

These two Timex campaigns are very good examples of *product benefits* that dramatize how the brand meets the consumer's needs... plus *consumer benefits* that speak to the user's idealization of self. The ads in both campaigns position Indiglo as a brand in and of itself.

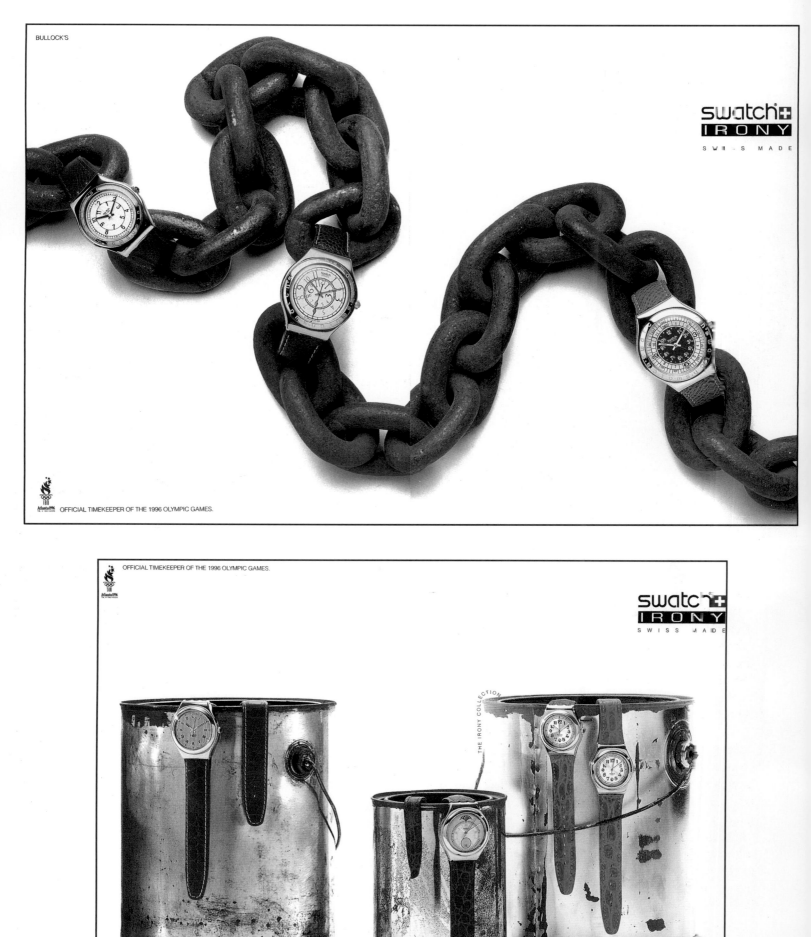

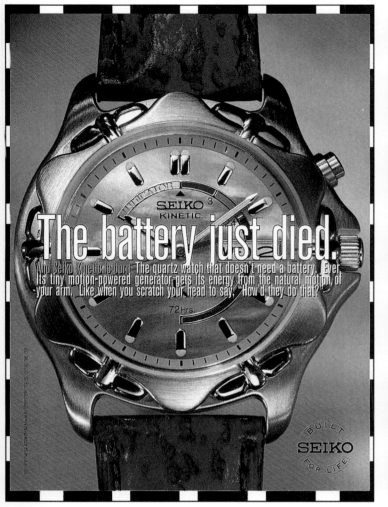

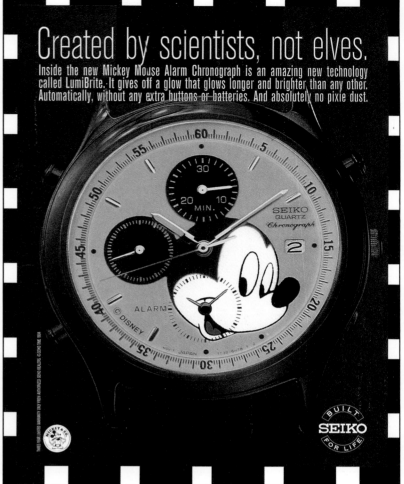

Time marches on. And on, and on. Fabulous designs wonderfully portrayed, Seiko and Swatch have captured life's time frame. In colorful designs, Swatch presents a variety of colorful alternatives upon which to build a dream. Seiko is tomorrow's dream come true today. Performance is the essence, distinctiveness the tonality of their advertising. In either case, the product is the central focal point of the celebration.

The "Swatch Irony" campaign brings Swatch's plastic image into a definitive new era of full metal. They have created a strong visual metaphor with a touch of "irony". Swatch's brand character communicates the values of this new collection that are most significant to their target consumers.

Seiko's "Built For Life" campaign provides relevant information about key product features that meet primary consumer needs and wants. However, the type is hard to read and might miss the target if they are not drawn in by the visual and/or headline.

WHAT WORKS IN

Sports & Fitness

FASHION

ADVERTISING

The Air Max² Sweep
tennis shoe with
dual pressure Air-Sole
cushioning by Nike.

The use of visual metaphors has a long tradition in advertising. To work, the visual must be instantly understandable, possibly funny or clever, and intrinsically related to the product. The Nike Air Max2 tennis shoe says "We'll do better than walking on air." Replete with images of the soft, cushiony equipment of our lives, this ad promises more than comfort, it promises the security and closeness of your teddy bear. Now that's visualizing a product benefit!

The Air Max2 running shoe ad zeroes in on the consumer who wants "to feel good" doing the team-thing. This may be sending mixed messages to high-schoolers who, as the visual indicates, may be more performance-oriented. Would they characterize the range of their wants and needs as hedonism? Does this consumer know what a hedonist is?

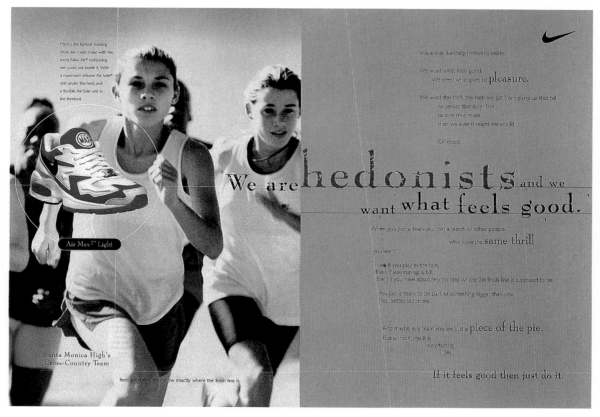

Timberland has capitalized on a reputation for rugged performance footwear to develop a line-extension strategy into outerwear. The advertising campaigns have always focused on a theme which links Timberland with the product benefit of protection from the elements. This current campaign maintains the Timberland identity by placing us in the extreme environments for which these products are made.

The character of the brand strategy is what makes this work. It's not "Man against the elements," rather it's "Man and Timberland with the elements". Nature isn't something to be conquered, with Timberland, it is to be participated in.

These are specific products that require more information. For example: cars, computers, and rugged outdoor/wilderness equipment and clothing. Without being dry, Timberland's approach is informative — with helpful details, enthusiastic — with the feel of adventure. The customers in this target market want and need products that are built "so nothing can stop them". They are willing to read more in preparation for this investment in high performance equipment.

Every element in Timberland's ads works toward sending the same message. They speak with one voice. The headline sets the stage; the body copy delivers the necessary details; the product photo-inserts visualize the copy; the "nature" photos put the reader within the great outdoors. The logo is always Timberland's rugged label. The slogan completes the picture: "Boots, shoes, clothing. Wind, water, earth and sky."

THERE ARE TIMES WHEN YOUR OWN SKIN ISN'T ENOUGH.

The point of our revealing photograph isn't to prove you should cover your butt with clothing when it snows.

It's to dramatize the fact that your skin does some wonderful things to keep you comfortable in extreme conditions. And so does our

skin, the incomparably protective leathers we use in Timberland® boots, shoes and clothing.

Consider the four pieces of durable Timberland gear pictured in this ad. Although each has a different use, they share a common foundation in the quality of leather used in their construction. Hide that's hand-picked for best results during the waterproofing process. And for natural coloration that weathers handsomely over time.

As its name suggests, the Iditarod™ Super Boot comes out of our many years of experimental

work outfitting mushers who compete in the annual blizzard-whipped 1,049-mile sled dog race stretching from Anchorage to Nome, Alaska.

With the Iditarod as our testing lab, we've proven that the waterproof leathers and 800-gram Thinsulate® insulation in this boot can stand up to anything in North America.

And even though you wouldn't wear our

Litchfield Bomber in a sled dog race, it will show you our long-standing ability to make waterproof leather as comfortable in a cloudburst as on a day when there isn't a cloud in the sky.

Likewise, our Weatherbuck Wingtips will take you to the office on a stormy day with feet as dry and warm as if you were wearing the toughest

Timberland boots. In fact, the method we use to waterproof these shoes comes directly from our boot-building repertoire. Over twenty years of industry leadership. No shortcuts and no compromises.

Lastly, our name wouldn't be Timberland if our fall offering didn't include a handsewn chukka boot for rugged wear, rain or shine. You get the double comfort of genuine handsewn construction plus a waterproof system built around a Gore-Tex® fabric bootie.

It's been a million years since the skin you were born with was forced to endure the planet's wildest extremes.

Not to worry. Use ours.

For more information about Timberland boots, shoes and clothing, call 1-800-445-5545.

Timberland

BOOTS, SHOES, CLOTHING, WIND, WATER, EARTH AND SKY.

OUR NAME IS MUD.

To most makers of footwear and apparel, mud is a dirty word.

Not to us. The way we see it, bad weather builds character. And if you've ever seen the character lines in a well-used Timberland® boot, you know what we mean.

What makes our boots (and all Timberland leather gear) age so proudly is the interaction of the elements in all their force with the finest materials the earth can provide.

Take the three pieces of rugged, versatile footwear shown on these pages. One is our signature, the timeless waterproof boot for all-around rugged use. Two is our handsewn Trekker, lined with a Gore-Tex® fabric bootie for waterproof comfort on the trail under any and all conditions.

And three is our well-known Weatherbuck, which combines classic

The eruption of Mount St. Helens in 1980 created a volcanic mud flow that moved as fast as a sea of cars going 50 m.p.h.

casual shoe styling with the no-compromise waterproof technology perfected in our boots, an ideal choice for work or weekends. All three look and feel as great when the mud is flying as when the sun is shining. So does our Iditarod™ 3-in-1 storm coat. To create it, we spent years working with Alaska's top mushers. And although you may never encounter Yukon-sized precipitation, you'll find its composition ideal for fending off the extremes of turbulence found in much of the North American continent. Specifically, its quilted inner jacket with Primaloft® insulation and nylon shell with waterproof, breathable Gore-Tex laminate.

Wind, rain, mud and slush are a normal part of the world we live in.

It's life — so make sure you dress for the occasion. Just call 1-800-445-5545 for a more complete look at Timberland boots, shoes and clothing.

Here's mud in your eye.

Timberland

BOOTS, SHOES, CLOTHING, WIND, WATER, EARTH AND SKY.

Just because the situation calls for a smaller pack doesn't mean you need one less technical. Hot Shot from The North Face.

There are a lot of trips that don't require your full-sized pack. Quick route-finding excursions. A full day of ski mountaineering. Hiking to an out-of-the-way climbing site. What you do need is the Hot Shot—a small, technical pack. The Hot Shot offers a divided front compartment, perfect for double water bottles.

It has compression straps specially spaced for ski bindings, as well as sternum and lower lash straps. The Hot Shot also gives you a padded back and shoulder pads.

And you literally can't beat the bulletproof bottom material. So, technically, you shouldn't be without the Hot Shot.

The terrain and sandstone in southern Utah are famous for the demands they put on outdoor enthusiasts and their gear. Here Andy Gillis day hikes in Arches National Park. The North Face makes a wide range of packs, tents, sleeping bags and clothing for all kinds of serious outdoor pursuits. For the dealer nearest you, or to receive a free catalog, call 1-800-384-FACE, ext. 21. Photo: Brian Bailey.

The let's-talk-your-language tone of this North Face campaign mirrors the medium it appeared in… Outside Magazine. The readers of such focused magazines are used to the technical jargon and references to the outdoor experience. Featuring well-known outdoor performers enhances the professional performance characteristics of the product.

The visuals and highly informative copy emphasize the product and the product-in-use. They provide their targeted segment with an experiential moment that whets the appetite for adventure but is also calculated to produce a bonding-with-the-brand. The message is — North Face will come through and so will you.

At 20,000' the sun offers only a false hope of heat, the cold hunts you like a crazed animal, and the Gore DryLoft fabric and 700 fill goose down in our Baltoro jacket may be your only refuge in this beautiful, icy hell.

It's in places like Vinson, Pangma, K2 and Cerro Torre that you find a different kind of cold. A relentless cold demanding a special respect. That's why we incorporated the baffled construction from our expedition sleeping bags into our Baltoro jacket. To eliminate cold spots, we hand-fill the ultimate in performance-to-weight insulation, 700 fill goose down into the Baltoro's 33 separate chambers. And the Baltoro is rugged enough to perform as a true piece of mountaineering outerwear. We accomplished this by using Gore DryLoft fabric, a thin-membrane, highly water- and wind-resistant fabric, more than twice as breathable as Gore-Tex fabric, yet extremely durable. We added Supplex Tactel on the shoulders and forearms for abrasion resistance, articulated the elbows, and gave it a full-length, two-way zipper and baffled, detachable hood. Cold? What cold?

Nameless Tower is several oxygen-deprived pitches above the Baltoro glacier in Pakistan's Karakoram region. Nameless may be its name, but the climbers who have attempted to ascend the tower have some pretty specific names for the weather. As Greg Child put it, "On a good day, you could climb it in a T-shirt. On a bad day, you could die." The North Face makes a wide range of clothing, packs, tents and sleeping bags for all kinds of serious outdoor pursuits. For the dealer nearest you, or to receive a free catalog, call 1-800-384-FACE, ext. 23. Photo: Galen Rowell.

Getting here was impossible. Tomorrow will likely be more difficult. Fortunately you'll sleep tonight thanks to your Snowshoe bag's Polarguard insulation and revolutionary new fabrics.

The weather is about as predictable as, well, the weather. That's why, if you're a serious mountaineer or backcountry hiker, the Snowshoe with Polarguard® HV is your bag. We use Polarguard HV because it's an extremely durable, continuous filament fiber that won't tear or separate like the synthetic fill used in other bags. The Snowshoe is rated to 0° and, like all bags from The North Face, takes advantage of our shingled construction to eliminate cold spots. It also combines our unique water- and wind-resistant Super Microfiber shell with our flannel-soft, heat-regulating ThermaStat℠ lining to give you incredible, all-night comfort. We could go on and on about our contoured hood, roomy foot box and two-way ventilating zipper, but by now you're probably...Zzzzzzzz.

The photo (left) shows alpinists Greg Child and Conrad Anker bivouacked at The Enclosure on Grand Teton. They've spent more time at high altitude than most airline pilots. Here they contemplate the next day's ascent from the comfort of their North Face Polarguard bags. Along with the Snowshoe, The North Face makes a wide range of sleeping bags, tents, packs and clothing for all kinds of serious outdoor pursuits. For the dealer nearest you, or to receive a free catalog, please call 1-800-384-FACE, ext. 45. Photo: Chris Noble

THE NORTH FACE

With its 3-layer Gore-Tex fabric, fully taped seams, integrated hood, zippered underarm vents, roomy cut and full front zipper with double storm flaps, you'd expect our Climb Light shell to weigh more than 20 oz. But it doesn't.

The dilemma is to pack light enough to make the assault yet carry enough gear for a margin of safety. That's why every one of the 20 ounces in our Climb Light™ shell has a job to do. We start with a rugged three-layer Gore-Tex® fabric that eliminates the need for a lining. Then we hot-tape every seam. The result, Gore's Extreme Wet Weather rating and an incredible function-to-weight ratio. But weight isn't everything. That's why we designed Climb Light with a long, loose and forgiving cut, allowing technical moves and room for layering. We integrated an adjustable hood and visor into the shell. And the full-length, two-way front zipper and extra-long underarm zippers both feature double storm flaps. For the performance of a technical jacket with the weight of a shell, don't get caught without Climb Light.

Alpinist and author Greg Child is pictured above wearing a Climb Light shell on a recent climb. Greg often takes along our gear on high-altitude climbs throughout the world. Along with Climb Light, The North Face makes a wide range of clothing, tents, sleeping bags and packs for all kinds of serious outdoor pursuits. For the dealer nearest you, or to receive a free catalog, call 1-800-384-FACE, ext 45. Photo: Chris Noble.

GORE-TEX
Outerwear
Gore-Tex is a Trademark of W.L. Gore & Associates, Inc.

THE NORTH FACE

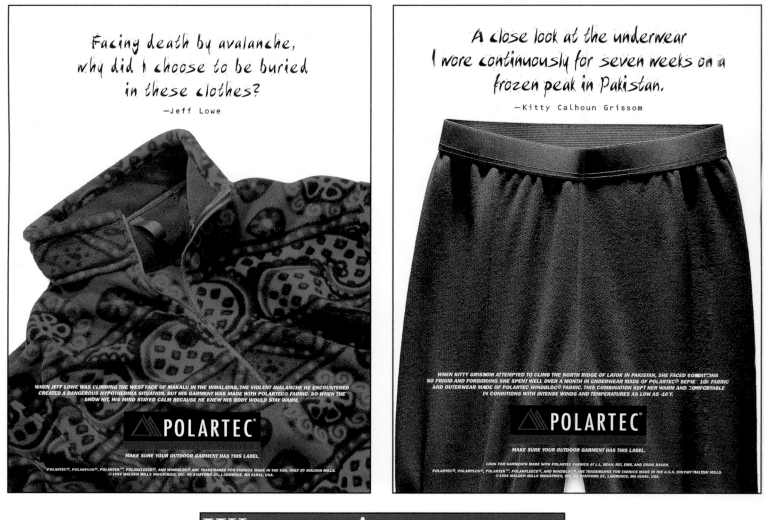

The use of testimonials from respected sources is blended with humorous ironies in the Polartec campaign. The typography in the headlines is stylized handwriting "signed" by these adventurers. They are designed to achieve reader attention. Polartec is using this lighter and decidedly more fashion-oriented approach to convince outdoor activists that performance and pulchritude are tactically compatible.

The Polartec ads are aimed at the urban outdoors type who may be as concerned with making a fashion statement as they are with surviving in the remote.

The Marmot ad has a lot to say about product attributes and its brand's character. It sort of mixes its message with its not too clear ramble between the dangers of the slippery slope and the hazards of the maleficent mall.

So, whose warranties are they endorsing in their headline? Is "Marmot for life"… the brand whose warranties have lived up to the consumer's expectations? How about really saying so — and showing us a picture of the Alpine Lightweight Jacket at least as large as the "great" in the headline?

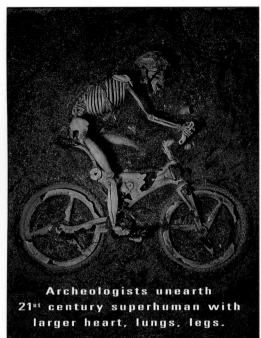

Archeologists unearth
21st century superhuman with
larger heart, lungs, legs.

"Vetta Man" found.

MOAB DIG, UTAH
MAY 8, 8994 A.D.
The well-preserved remains of a highly evolved man were found mounted on a bicycle today. This remarkable find is providing archeologists with clues to 21st century "Vetta Man's" life.

The first "Vetta Man" was found in Moab, Utah last May. So named because of the "Vetta" inscription on his helmet and protective eyewear, "Vetta Man" has shattered current perceptions of Pre-Thermal* Man.

Pre-Thermal Man, or "Porcine (pig-like) Man", was believed to have avoided physical exercise, except for using his fingers on computer keypads, TV remotes and consuming french fried potatoes. He carried 35% of his body weight in fat, inhaled smoldering sticks, had an average life span of 50 years, and rode in inefficient four-wheeled machines.

Evidently, a different species existed at the same time. "Vetta Man" cycled extensively on bicycles, seemed to have only 5% body fat and was extremely powerful. Studies indicate his average life span was 90 years, nearly twice that of sedentary "Porcine Man". Other bones and bicycle parts found at the dig indicate that "Vetta Men" traveled in communities that included women and children, all competing for the lead position as they hurtled onwards.

Upon examining the Moab cyclist's oversized rib cage, it is apparent that "Vetta Man" had larger lungs than "Porcine Man". They probably mutated over time due to the massive amounts of oxygen his body required to endure physical hardships. His leg bones were overly developed too, probably a result of constant pedaling over mountainous terrain.

The discovery of an object attached to the handlebar supports this theory. This device, called the C 15, has a dual line display screen and is apparently a cycle computer. Scientists speculate that "Vetta Man" used the C 15 to calculate both his average and maximum speed and measure the distance he traveled.

A lightweight saddle found at the site probably cushioned "Vetta Man's" hindquarters during bumpy stretches. Reassembling the saddle, labeled TT Carbon TriShock, revealed an ingenious three-point shock absorption system made from extraordinarily strong carbon fibers sheathed in steel. The saddle weighed a slight 141 grams, which places it among the lightest artifacts recovered from the Pre-Thermal Age, raising questions about the technological sophistication of that era.

A protective headdress was also found. While similar to the one discovered at the original Moab dig, this new discovery had more holes and a sophisticated style. Scientists now speculate these openings kept "Vetta Man" cool during cycling and believe the sophisticated design designated this "Vetta Man" as a leader of the tribe.

An unbreakable U-shaped steel retaining device inscribed with the title "Revenge" and protective, aerodynamic eyewear were also unearthed. Anthropologists speculate that "Vetta Man" used the "Revenge" to protect his bicycle from thieves and scavengers while the advanced eyewear protected him from airborne hazards and the invisible solar radiation of the heavily polluted and dangerous Pre-Thermal environment.

Scientists have many answers, but questions still remain about Pre-Thermal "Vetta Man". Was he racing for sport or trying to escape from "Porcine Man"? Or had he simply discovered a fitter lifestyle that helped him survive longer? Researchers hope that a promising find recently uncovered in Old California holds the clues.

*It's common knowledge that the Thermal Age lasted from 2090 A.D. to 3440 A.D. The effect of the ever-expanding ozone hole, combined with the depletion of the rain forests, caused the earth's surface to heat up and melt down. 99% of life was wiped out. By around the 61st century, the human race had reestablished itself and civilization was flourishing.

C 15 Cycle Computer. (Simulated image.)

"Vetta Man's" vented headdress protected him from injury.

"Revenge" bicycle locking device.

The lightweight saddle bore the inscription "TT TriShock Carbon". (Simulated image.)

Aerodynamic eye wear. (Simulated image.)

VETTA ONLY THE FITTEST SURVIVE.

EASTPAK MADE IN U.S.A.

Guaranteed for life. Maybe longer.

Journeys   The Sports Authority   Sharon Luggage

In sports fitness being lean and mean is a notable goal. What's leaner than a skeleton or meaner than a piranha? Eastpack has adopted a somewhat gruesome theme, that your backpack will probably last longer than you will. The emphasis here is on durability in extreme conditions. They have chosen to let the visual image tell most of the tale. Their logo (fabric label) and their slogan tell the rest — "Guaranteed for life. Maybe longer." This is an important product promise as well as clever copy.

The Jansport and Vetta ads, while seemingly dissimilar, share important characteristics. Both are aimed squarely at Generation X'ers and both utilize a very entertaining soft-sell approach.

Vetta's use of humor is poking fun at the current day habits of the man who doesn't exercise. They present their serious equipment product in a clever future-meets-past story that also establishes the predicted longevity of this brand/company.

After the tongue-in-cheek headline and subhead, Jansport presents a very straight forward message in the target market's own style: "This is our pack. It holds a lot… And now we'd like you to buy some of it." Remember the last lesson or rule in salesmanship is to "always ask for the sale". Their slogan also implies the target market's need for escape — "Get out while you can."

THE PUFFER FISH HAS A TOUGH EXTERIOR AND IS ABLE TO BLOW ITSELF UP TO FIVE TIMES ITS NORMAL SIZE.

SAME STORY. ONLY THE PACK DOESN'T SUCK.

THIS IS OUR PACK. IT HOLDS A LOT. IT LASTS A LONG TIME. IT'S NOT A BAD PILLOW EITHER. WE'VE SPENT MORE THAN 25 YEARS OUTDOORS FIGURING OUT HOW TO MAKE STUFF LIKE THIS. AND NOW WE'D LIKE YOU TO BUY SOME OF IT. CALL 1-800-552-6776 TO FIND OUT MORE.

CIRCLE 136 ON ADVERTISER INFORMATION CARD

JANSPORT
GET OUT WHILE YOU CAN

EASTPAK

Guaranteed for life. Maybe longer.

Belk   Millers Outpost   Just For Feet

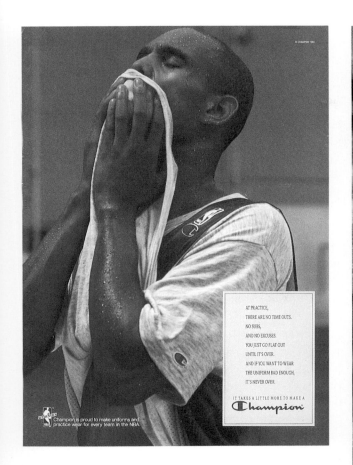

Product benefits linked to the lifestyle of the target market is the strategy adopted by the Jansport ads. This is a fine example of the product-as-companion, relationship marketing. Visuals which show the product in action with the user underscoring the relationship.

In the other ads the main appeal is use of the product by professionals. The Champion ads feature haiku-like copy combined with a bold, attention-getting visual. Champion's approach is to connect with the feelings of playing the game — from the sweating, aching participant's point of view.

The Russell Athletic ad does not use specific products to support its message about durability. The visual and copy say little about the product attributes that contribute to its performance. The message is more institutional in its attempt to build the reputation of the brand as a supplier of professional team uniforms that can take professional-level punishment. Quality by association is Russell's strategy to build brand character.

Reebok has always positioned itself as a lifestyle and lifestage sports shoe. The strategy focuses on consumer benefits promised to those who venture to the "Planet Reebok". The target market is being directly addressed with emotional appeals that are dramatized by visuals that show the consumer working at it. The message reflects a knowledge of the consumer's mindset as evidenced by its very intimate copy approach. The message attempts to communicate that Reebok is the thinking woman's choice for athletic footwear. The models used and the visuals of the product-in-use reflect that this campaign is aimed at the 30-something to 50-something woman. This campaign is targeted to a consumer segment that sees individuality and independence as a measure of personal achievement.

The Nike ad uses a brilliant visual concept to dramatize a product benefit for maximum effect. Nike offers a visually documented guarantee of what won't happen to their air resistance tennis shoe. They cleverly use this attribute to point to its other features. Nike's execution of copy and art is an excellent example of how to make the "creative connection" between words and pictures.

The ACG Nike ad makes the same "creative connection". The MTV-style typography says "big sharp teeth" in an effective sync with the "product-as-hero". There is no doubt where you use this shoe, and why it will do the job.

Reebok

There's a part of us that believes

we can always be better.

Stronger.

Smarter.

More beautiful.

So when you work out,

work out that part first.

STEP REEBOK℠ CREATOR GIN MILLER WORKS OUT IN THE REEBOK AEROSTEP PRO. A VERSATILE SHOE WITH A GRAPHLITE® ARCH THAT DOESN'T TRADE WEIGHT FOR SUPPORT. PERFECT FOR AEROBICS AND STEP REEBOK℠ CLASS, IT MIGHT EVEN STRENGTHEN YOUR BELIEFS.

Reebok believes in the athlete. In all of us.

PLANET REEBOK

FOR MORE INFORMATION ABOUT REEBOK PRODUCTS FOR WOMEN, CALL 1-800-843-4444.

IF THIS WERE A WOODLAND CREATURE IT WOULD BE SLEEK, NIMBLE, FRIENDLY AND HAVE BIG SHARP TEETH

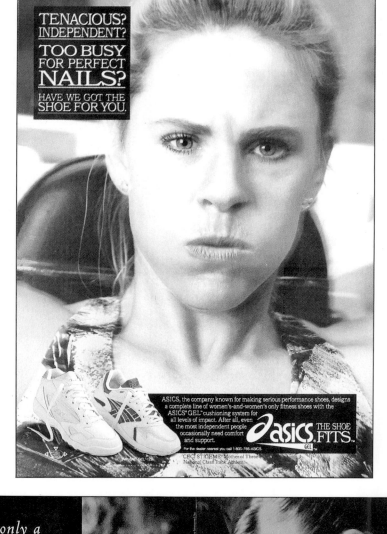

Asics invites consumers to pick their own psychographic characteristics. This is an example of market segmentation by behavior. The twist here is that the behaviors are not necessarily nice, which is fine if your market doesn't care about being nice.

After grabbing the reader's attention with these arresting headlines, Asics continues the theme in the body copy. They have chosen to use "real people" athletes to lend credibility to their offer — mother — national class track athlete; lawyer — national class marathoner; American record holder — mile run. Without using their voices, they are endorsing Asics.

Avia uses a woman's perspective on sports to present its 695 aerobic shoe. Their strategy is to associate their product with an "everybody wins" "how could you lose" approach.

In all of these ads, the reality of putting the reader inside the positive feelings of exercising and running in quality shoes, specifically engineered for these activities, is evident and well executed.

The ads on this page share a similar strategy and execution. The art, graphics and layout all speak to a young, serious runner who considers a running shoe as performance equipment. The product is featured visually with the benefits highlighted in the copy.

The rock and roll style headline, "True Love Never Did Run Smooth" is the antithesis of the strategy of the ads on the opposite page. These ads use a factual copy approach to focus on the consumer. The target market is getting to an age where the concern moves from performance to comfort and protection.

Technology plays a major role in the science of designing the best athletic shoes. The key is to draw the reader's attention into the ad so the copy will be read with interest — building a desire to buy this brand and/or shoe.

Although the reader would not see these ads together as we review them here, the competition is fierce in this product category and the consumer is looking for the shoes that will answer their very specific needs. Each company attempts to provide the answer or to be the solution to the readers' problems.

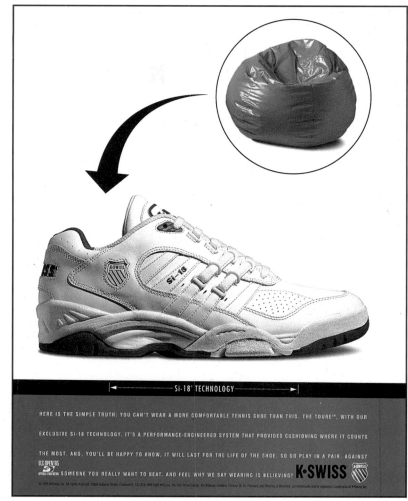

Si-18® TECHNOLOGY

Unlike his
Aztec ancestors,
German Silva
SACRIFICES
nothing.

To prepare for competition, the Aztecs made offerings to their gods. NY Marathon winner German Silva has found a more civilized way: he trains in Fila Sky Runner 2A shoes with patented 2A Technology. So when Silva prepares, he doesn't sacrifice a thing.

You see, feet want two things from a running shoe -- cushioning and stability. And the Sky Runner 2A provides both. The secret is Fila's 2A Technology. A matrix of posts within an air chamber, 2A not only limits lateral movement for superior stability, but also softens impact.

That means runners like Silva can keep even the most torturous training regimens. Without giving up a thing.

Sky Runner 2A

FILA
change the GAME

WITH ANY OTHER SHOE, THERE'D PROBABLY BE AN INJURY BY NOW.

Etonic
BUILT
1-800-84-ETONIC

Quick — which campaigns have the hard-sell and which have the soft-sell ads? The Avia ads certainly look hard-sell but that's due to the edginess of the highly stylized illustrations. They're really lifestyle-oriented with the product playing an integral role. The visuals are designed to show product features and to promise benefits to a segment that has a devil-may-care sense of their own immortality.

The Salomon ad with its almost Zen-like photo contains body copy that could have been written by a good shoe salesman.

The Timberland ad lets the reader virtually try on the shoe in its action shot. We sort of wonder whether the wearer would easily "blow through rock" with the laces untied? The headline and visual suggest product benefits and innovations in design that range from "blowing through rock like a human jackhammer" to not slipping on the slick ones. Is the Toporelief out-sole capable of both these functions? Convince us.

Street Slammer," about $40.   ©1995 L.A. Gear, Inc.

Products that put you in motion need to be set in motion by their layout, art, copy, and typography. Outstanding performance is the major appeal that begins to move customers to buy athletic footwear.

Nike and Reebok have conditioned this market to appreciate shoe design and foot care as a science. LA Gear plays on the edge of this engineered product approach, but keeps its foot in *fashion* footwear too.

These layouts indicate jumping and motion, and use graphics in the same way as in motion picture credits and story lines that crawl up the big screen. It's a different approach that adds entertainment appeal to product information.

VANS targets its brand to a segment of the market whose attitude is a rejection of heavy exercise. They position VANS with a humorous approach. "Vacation," "can't tell time," "picking up girls," and "wind in your toe hair," are attention-getting visual and verbal metaphors. The copy speaks to the less-than-serious dudes surfing the surf—or the net.

Hepburn Plaid," about $20.   ©1995 L.A. Gear.

Life is a three-inch heel with rubber sole vacations.

Available at Burdine's

There's a time for work and a time for play. These shoes can't tell time.

For a catalog call 1 (800) VANS 800

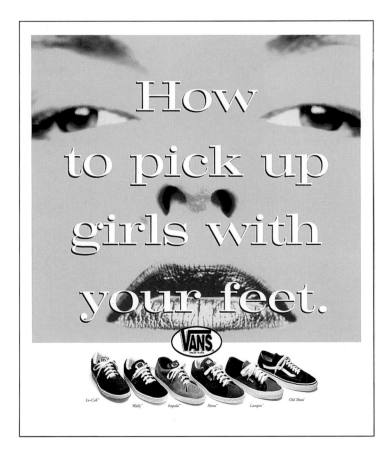

How to pick up girls with your feet.

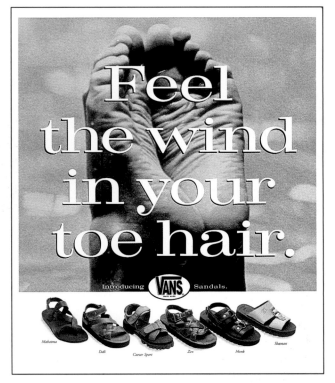

Feel the wind in your toe hair.

Introducing Vans Sandals.

Another piece of unsolicited advice on Planet Reebok.

The most
brilliant elements
in DESIGN
are often
the most supportive.

See.

Double Cross

Inspired by the soaring strength of La Saint Chapelle's flying buttresses, we came up with yet another revolutionary idea: rather than conventional lace-up design, why not multi-functional support straps. Not only would they literally lock feet into position, they'd provide more efficient support for the ankle. The result, as any cross-trainer can tell you, is clearly inspiring.

FILA
change
the GAME™

©1995 FILA USA, Inc.

It has been said that "the medium is the message"…
Here we see two Reebok ads with messages designed
to speak to two totally different audiences.

The ad at left was placed in *Outdoor*, a magazine for
outdoor adventurers. The ad's entire focus is on the
outdoor activities of this magazine's readers and the
Reebok AmaZone product's use. The layout art, type
and graphics speak to the mind, body, and soul (or is
that sole?) of this target market.

The other Reebok ad shown below was in *Martha
Stewart Living*, a women's home magazine. This ad
provides valuable information about how the right
shoe can help soothe the total mind and body of a
hardworking, tired woman, similarly to reflexology!
Reebok presents a bold visual/verbal connection
between the foot's reflex zones and their shoe design's
technology for relieving tension.

Fila provides a unique visual to sell the "support"
selling point in *Details*, a men's magazine.

Etonic zeros in on the runner's main injury zone—
the knee. Their technology and scientific design adds
believability to the message in *Running* magazine.

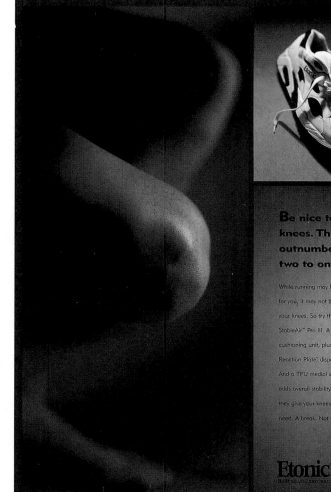

**Be nice to your
knees. They
outnumber you
two to one.**

While running may be good
for you, it may not be good for
your knees. So try the Etonic
StableAir™ Pro III. A StableAir™
cushioning unit, plus a Dynamic
Reaction Plate,™ disperses shock.
And a TPU medial support plug
adds overall stability. Together,
they give your knees what they
need. A break. Not a sprain.

Etonic
Built so you can last.

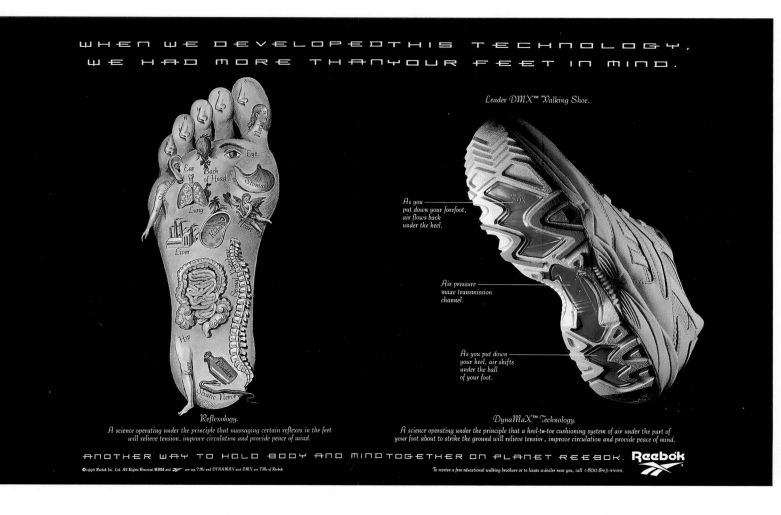

WHEN WE DEVELOPED THIS TECHNOLOGY,
WE HAD MORE THAN YOUR FEET IN MIND.

Leader DMX™ Walking Shoe.

As you
put down your forefoot,
air flows back
under the heel.

Air pressure
maze transmission
channel.

As you put down
your heel, air shifts
under the ball
of your foot.

Reflexology.
A science operating under the principle that massaging certain reflexes in the feet
will relieve tension, improve circulation and provide peace of mind.

DynaMaX™ Technology.
A science operating under the principle that a heel-to-toe cushioning system of air under the part of
your foot about to strike the ground will relieve tension, improve circulation and provide peace of mind.

ANOTHER WAY TO HOLD BODY AND MIND TOGETHER ON PLANET REEBOK. **Reebok**

To receive a free educational walking brochure or to locate a dealer near you, call 1-800-843-4444.

HEAVY-HITTERS HAVE ALWAYS WORN PINSTRIPES.

NOTHING SAYS POWER LIKE PINSTRIPES. THE FILA HERITAGE COLLECTION AS REINTERPRETED BY ANDREI MEDVEDEV. A NEW LINE OF POWER HAS BEEN DRAWN.———▶ CHANGE THE GAME.™ **FILA**

KENT STEFFES, WORLD BEACH VOLLEYBALL CHAMPION, RELAXING OFF THE COURT IN HIS POLAR FLEECE AND DELPHI LEATHER RUNNING SHOES — FROM FILA.

CHANGE THE GAME.™ **FILA**

Is it fashion or function? How is a consumer to know? Simple, the advertiser tells them. This is the essence of a positioning strategy and it's exemplified in these two campaigns.

Pinstripe power from the Fila Heritage Collection will intimidate your opponent on the tennis court. The right footwear is essential to fashionable relaxation off the court. This is Fila's approach to brand positioning. And their slogan, "change the game," is a consumer benefit message to the personal positioning of the potential customer. Fila's insight that athletic apparel is as acceptable as "fashion" may be where this market is going.

Nike is all about attitude. The just-do-it philosophy is a challenge which appeals to a market that wouldn't be caught dead lying on a hammock or watching old movies. Nike also knows all athletes need to be motivated. They play the coach inside of the athlete's head — taunting, advising, encouraging, pushing, chiding… Just-Do-It! Nike owns this philosophy and no longer needs to put in in every ad.

When you don't wear your name on your jersey, you have to find other ways to make people remember it.

If your teeth still chatter, it's fear.

There's no expressed fashion statement here, nor should there be. Nike maintains consistent identity with its "just-do-it" philosophical approach that doesn't vary from category to category. The visuals create an experience that the athletically-empowered consumer can virtually feel — because the characters in the ads are showing it in their faces and saying it in their body language.

It's the product-as-hero and the product in use — more real than pretty. The Nike campaigns are effective in communicating with the consumer because they focus on the inside of a person while demonstrating the action on the outside.

This is apparel for war, not the mall. If you're serious you'd better take heed because your competitor is training right now and guess what he's wearing?

Somewhere there's a nice, sunny place with warm breezes and shady palms where all the second-place guys train.

Forget about biodegradable tees.
Maybe what this world needs is a biodegradable putter.

Then, when it misbehaves badly,
you don't even have to take it home to punish it.

You can just leave it lying there, on the green.

And you can walk away and abandon it,
right where it abandoned you.

And over time, with the help of rain, sun and wind,
it'll slowly dissolve to nothing.

Just like your putting game.

But it won't be a total loss.

Because maybe it'll have a few nutrients left in it,
and they'll return to the earth, slowly but surely.

And the earthworms will feast on it,
like a big all-you-can-eat buffet.

And those earthworms will grow big and mighty and strong.

And, if there's any justice in the world, those earthworms
will rise up, one clear moonlit night, and attack that greenskeeper
who made your two-foot putt curl to the right like that.

*Here's another thing that's grown big
and mighty and strong. The Odyssey putter.
Last year on the Senior PGA Tour,
we were number one in victories,
number one in player usage and number one
in money earned. This year we're way
out front again. A big reason: see that black
trapezoid in the face? It's a soft material
called Stronomic, for incredible feel.
All you've got to do is pick one up and try it.
Then you can bury your other putters out
in the back yard. 1-800-437-5662.*

⬤ **ODYSSEY GOLF**

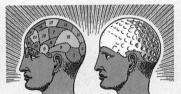

Remember, golf is not brain surgery.

It's harder.

A person can actually learn brain surgery.

A person can never really learn golf.

There are 4,501 brain surgeons in the U.S.,
with a median income of $500,000.

There are about 50 golfers in the U.S. that
make $500,000 or more.

On a brain surgeon, it's the eyes that
usually go first.

On a golfer, the brain can pretty much go
any day of the week, followed, in quick order,
by everything else.

Brain surgeons have, at most, 8 or 10 people
watching them.

Golfers have anywhere from 3 to 45 million
people watching them.

On bad days, a brain surgeon may sit back
and dream about retiring to play golf.

On bad days, which can occur anytime, a
golfer may sit back and dream about visiting
a brain surgeon. Hey, you've tried everything
else. Maybe they've figured out that
transplant thing by now.

*This'll take a load off your mind.
The Odyssey putter.
In just over two years, it's become the
most popular putter on the Senior PGA Tour.
And it's the first putter to ever surpass Ping.
That mysterious black spot in the face is a
big reason why. It's called Stronomic.
It's softer than other materials,
for incredible feel and flawless roll.
To feel what we mean, you'll just have to try it.
Call us at 1-800-437-5662.
Then you can put the whole brain surgery thing
out of your mind once and for all.*

⬤ **ODYSSEY GOLF**

Brain surgeons, rocket scientists, entomology, what's going on here? Let's see, golfers are: absorbed with technology, frequently in professional occupations and truly believe they can buy a better game. Perfect for marketers.

But these ads may go too many rounds before making their point. For some, they distract the reader's attention away from the equipment where it belongs. The Odyssey ads are particularly off the mark in their attempt to bond with the golfer. If you have a point to make about a product's U.S.P., then make it directly and reinforce it with believable copy and art.

For others, the humor and science may just add that extra something that keeps them reading and interested enough in the brand and its attributes to call the "1-800 pro shops".

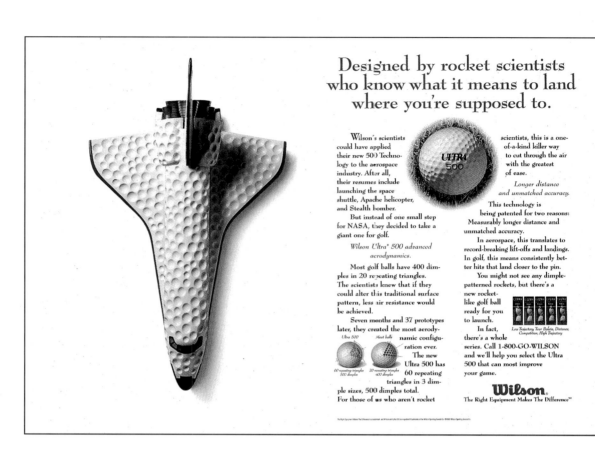

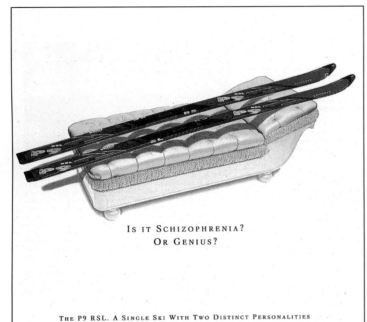

IS IT SCHIZOPHRENIA?
OR GENIUS?

THE P9 RSL. A SINGLE SKI WITH TWO DISTINCT PERSONALITIES

With its flexible segmented edges on the inside, the precise, exacting ski propels itself through a series of quick, tight turns in rapid succession. It seeks out the steeps and finds an almost perverse pleasure in bashing big, big bumps or carving up hard, hard snow. But change the skis from one foot to the other and a second

personality emerges instantly. The rigid, continuous edge is now on the inside and the turns are long and smooth. Its speed increases dramatically, yet it remains undisturbed, still under total control. Perhaps Freud never got it, but you can. *See your Völkl Dealer for both sides of the story.*

Völkl

German Engineering. American Style.

Völkl Sport America, W. Lebanon 392.

Look at the visuals, read the headlines and decide which campaign is more effective.

The Salomon ads are about product use, emotion and movement. They place the reader/skier in the product, on the slopes, in the snow. The Völkl ad is about symbol stretching. Having a split personality may imply that this ski offers two distinct traits — but it will have to be appreciated in order to pull the skier into the ad to get the point across. This may be a harder sell.

If all of the ski equipment ads, or those of Völkl's competitors, are producing full-color, dramatic action photography ads — this may create a difference that stands out from the crowd. If not — no contest.

RACING IS FULL OF ROUGH SPOTS.
SOME PEOPLE JUST GET OVER THEM FASTER.

THE SHOCK-ABSORBING SUSPENSION DRIVER.

When the going gets tough, the tough get Salomon Suspension Driver bindings. No useless gadgetry here. This breakthrough, 3-part binding system improves both ski and skier performance significantly (you don't need to race to feel it). Inside, a unique shock absorbing piston swallows up ruts, chatter marks and bruising terrain like the suspension on a car. Racers say it gives them the confidence to go even faster. The podium says they're right. The Suspension Driver. Designed to help you get over the ups and downs of racing, fast. *While no binding can guarantee absolute protection in every circumstance, we feel Salomon bindings help reduce the risk of injury. Ski within your limits.*

SALOMON

**WITHOUT THE RIGHT BOOTS,
MAYBE YOUR HANDS ARE TOGETHER BECAUSE
YOU'RE PRAYING.**

Precise, go-where-you're-aiming control. Without it, careening down glare ice, shear cliff race courses could leave you hoping there's a higher power out there. If so, the Salomon Integral Equipe 9.1 may be the answer to your prayers.

Its higher power transmission, sensitivity, fit, edge-to-edge quickness and turn acceleration are second to none. Which is why you see more and more coming in first – in racing and boot tests worldwide. The Salomon Integral Equipe 9.1. The new power in boots.

SALOMON

**SALOMON INTRODUCES A BOOT
YOU DON'T NEED PLASTIC GATES TO APPRECIATE.
WOOD ONES WILL DO NICELY.**

We admit it, we're crazy about racing. But we also know that for lots of people, a great time skiing has nothing to do with getting a great time. So we created Optima. The high performance hybrid boot that combines precise control and racing caliber power transmission with – dare we say it – comfort and easy on/off convenience.

So instead of spending time jamming your feet into vice-like race boots, you can be out jamming turns. The Optima and Optima Lady (designed specifically for women). A new breed of boot for a different breed of skier.

SALOMON

HARD TIMES ARE OVER.

Anyone can make a skate go a little faster. The question is, can anyone stop the darn things?

Well, yes. Introducing Oxygen. An absolute state-of-the-art collection of in-line skates with the world's first truly effective braking system.

It's our Power Braking System. A unique spring controlled heel brake activates an internal brake pad to slow the rear wheel. The result? Brake pressure is increased. Braking is smoother, and more controlled. Stops are shorter and safer.

But there's more. Our exclusive AutoRock system

provides instant wheel rockering. Without tools. With your skates on your feet.

Our vented monocoque shell and frame construction produces greater rigidity for increased power. While our hand-lasted, breathable liners have integrated flex panels for perfect fit. Considering we use ABEC-rated German bearings, aluminum spacers and Hyper and Kryptonics wheels, there really is nothing stopping us. Except, of course, our brake.

Our KR 03 is also available in a woman's skate. For details about all its cool details call 1-800-258-5020.

Our new skate brake will stop you just as quick, but it's much easier on your dental work.

Safety and comfort. Two selling points not usually associated with in-line skating. But here they are. Lots of factual copy and compelling visuals give the products in the Exotech and Koflach ads their brand identity and differentiation. The Exotech visual is easy for the skater to relate to. You know the maneuver. The brand difference is comfort along with performance, designed with the help of a U.S. Olympic speed skater.

Because of the layout, the close-up of a brick wall doesn't work as well with the headline in the Koflach Oxygen ad. If the claim is for a braking system that is as effective as the proverbial brick wall in making the stop — but smoother, why not visualize the positive of "the world's first truly effective braking system"? How about showing the product in use doing its thing?

Apparently this Headwinds Helmet campaign is taking the let's-talk-like-our customers approach. If the helmet is named "Splatter," throw some food at it, if it's "Shocker" some Frankenstein electrodes will do, if it's "Hothead," a blast furnace is cool. These ads say nothing about the product (until the footnote's mention of the certifications) but perhaps more about the person who would want to wear it.

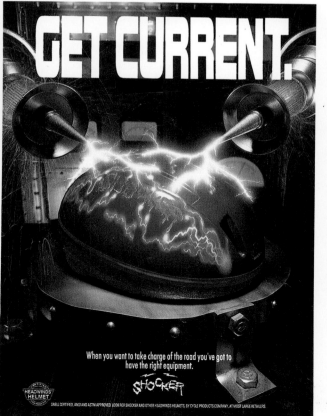

THE WORLD'S GREAT SKIERS HAVE ALWAYS HAD A SPIRITUAL CONNECTION TO THE MOUNTAINS.

This three-page ad presents Salomon's innovative product benefit — the "monocoque prolink." It is written and visualized in language that the skier understands. The message is designed to appeal to the skier's feeling for what is undoubtedly "their world," spiritually and environmentally. The tone of the message helps the reader to project what the product can contribute to their personal downhill performance.

In this double spread, Salomon proclaims its unique product difference by citing its influence on World Cup competition. The dynamic visuals and graphics support the copy that states "the way skis turn" will never be the same.

There is no doubt that much of the skier's excitement is enhanced by the nature of their special equipment and apparel. The opportunity to "suit-up" is part of what they believe is an unparalleled experience. Just think how the combination of textures, colors and patterns in this action shot speaks to the skier who sees this in the no-snow-days of August or September. Is it conceivable that their longing for the mountains and the slopes could stimulate an out-of-the-closet advance fashion show for the apparel and the equipment?

NOW THEY HAVE A 13 INCH, LONGITUDINAL, SELF-REGULATING, HIGH-AMPLITUDE, VISCO-ELASTIC CONNECTION TO THEM.

MONOCOQUE PROLINK. FULL CONTACT SKIING IS HERE. How do you top Monocoque? Monocoque Prolink. Technology that's turning the World Cup upside down by changing the way skis turn. Patented shock-absorbing arms, connected to regulators, move along the ski surface, actively swallowing shocks, adapting to changing terrain and pressing the ski firmly to the snow. Edge contact is extended from the tip to the tail. Steering and control are extended to a level this side of supernatural. Prolink Equipe 1S, Equipe 3S and Prolink EXP Demo. To learn more about Full Contact Skiing, contact your Salomon dealer. Or watch a World Cup race. **SALOMON**

WHAT WORKS IN

*C*osmetics & Beauty

FASHION

ADVERTISING

Take away its

OXYGEN

and what do you think would happen?

Just like your skin. If you want it to bloom again, you've got to give it what it needs.

Oxygen to help re-energize cells.

Concentrated moisturizers to keep skin smooth and firm.
Reduce the chance of wrinkles.

And defensive protection to diffuse environmental damage.
Before it gets you.

Just like nature, Monteil is sending help your way.
ACTIVANCE the remarkable new energy serum that revitalizes, moisturizes and protects your skin.

All in one step. All in two drops.

ACTIVANCE. THE ENERGY SERUM.

BEAUTY ❦ SCIENCE

MONTEIL
PARIS

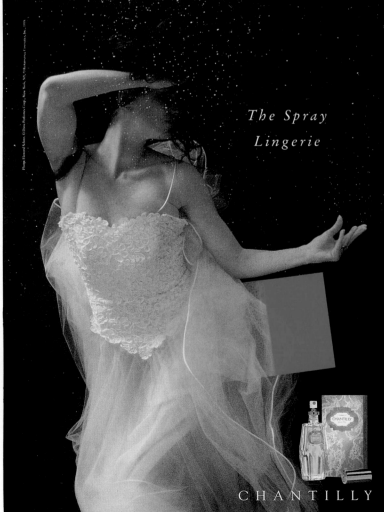

The Spray
Lingerie

CHANTILLY

Deci Dela

The new perfume from

NINA RICCI
PARIS
1-800-758-0081

FOLEY'S • FILENE'S • KAUFMANN'S
HECHT'S • FAMOUS BARR

Aromatics Elixir photographed for Clinique by Irving Penn. © Clinique Laboratories, Inc.

The world of cosmetics, fragrance and toiletries advertising has centered around self-idealization, fantasy, and more recently, science. Providing a unique reason-to-buy has become more critical especially in cosmetics and treatment products.

Monteil represents the trend toward scientific solutions to combat nature's effect on the skin. The reader is drawn in by the compelling life source—OXYGEN. The delicate flower and the soothing blue tones soften the scientific message while communicating its importance.

The three fragrance ads build their name recognition with tie-ins to other sources of pleasure—"The Spray Lingerie" featured on a model from an old master's painting; "Deci Dela" with fantasy butter-

flies that are Oh so French; and visual associations with ancient elixirs and potions from the past.

Without scent strips it is difficult to actually sell the fragrance. The key point must be to position the image of the product in the mind of the consumer.

Does she feel most sexy in her elegant, "Chantilly" lace nightgown?

Does she feel playful with and intrigued by French perfumes?

Is she an adventurer with travel and the discovery of lost cultures in her mind?

These are two very different approaches. They must be determined early on in the strategic positioning of the brand, and in the development of attributes and appeals that create the reasons to buy!

Fragrance advertising has rarely been about the actual product. Moreover it is designed to position the brand as the appropriate scent to induce the desired effect. These three ads use the same design techniques — full, dreamy photography to set the mood, product insets to show the actual bottle, simple and direct copy to match the visual.

Both of the copy lines: "The essence of being" and "Relax Your Mind   Enjoy Your Body" — are relevant to today's consumer attitudes. The inner self and the physical pleasures of life are related to what each of these fragrances claims to deliver.

Internal and external beauty are being given as the reasons to buy given by the advertiser. They should appeal to the target market.

"Il Bacio" is Italian for "The Kiss" — and we have all been treated to the romantic/sexy image of the Italian lover. (Notice the popularity of the award-winning movie "Il Postino" — "The Postman".) If this fragrance lives up to that image, the consumer may buy the Il Bacio fantasy and remain loyal to the brand as long as it fulfills its promise.

Stereotypes prevail in these ads. In "Boys like to experiment," the message allows that boys will be boys in their desire to mix the formulas for a new fragrance with an appealing chemistry. This ad will no doubt appeal to the mischievous boy in the young man who still likes to experiment. Catalyst is being targeted toward a specific consumer whose attitudes, lifestyle, and lifestage are reflected in this clever series ad.

Feminine elegance, beauty, and sweetness are the choice of Estée Lauder for its "pleasures" and "BEAUTIFUL" fragrances. Fragrance advertising must project the image the consumer represents or wishes to represent. This is done by strong imagery in the choice of specific themes that build on the product name. The vivid tone of each ad speaks to the target consumer through the coherent visual and verbal message.

Jean Paul Gaultier's "Haute Parfumerie" is a tribute to his position in the haute couture design world. He speaks with "one voice" throughout his clothing and fragrance campaigns. Image is the name of the game and that affects his choice of every element of the product through to the package design.

FROM THE HEART
OF AFRICA
COMES
A FRAGRANCE
TO CAPTURE
THE HEART
OF EVERY WOMAN.

Consumer segmentation provides advertisers with the opportunity to better target their audience with a more focused message. When a product is designed with an ethnic influence, such as "Ajee" by Revlon, the advertising must reflect the brand's character. This is strongly represented in this three page ad. The African theme is stated in the copy and visualized beautifully with the well-chosen model, African jewelry, clothing, background photo of an Acacia tree and the African veld. The product name, packaging graphics, speak with the same voice, delivering the same message about this exotic fragrance by Revlon.

WHITE LINEN
ESTĒE LAUDER

Fragrances are often associated with other tactile elements in our lives, such as flowing, soft or sexy fabrics. The touch and feel of fabrics can produce inner feelings about a mood or a setting — Here we see how the advertising can visually project the mood or feeling as it is positioned in the mind of the consumer — "White Linen" — provides the feeling of the softness of summer breezes along the sea shore, the smell of the soft sea air, the relaxed image of a dreamy vacation... and "Chantilly" — puts the consumer in mind of the boudoir, behind lace curtains — reminding us that this is "The Spray Lingerie" — don't leave home without it. These are not new fragrances so their main objective is to keep the name in front of their loyal customers, to build Brand Loyalty, and to continue to attract new customers.

CHANTILLY

THE SPRAY LINGERIE

Parfums Parquet's Chantilly™ Renaissance Cosmetics, Inc ©1994

INTRODUCING LIP INTENSITIES

CHANEL

LIP COLOUR COMES OUT TO PLAY
WITH FOUR FABULOUS FINISHES AND COOL COLOUR. HOT OFF THE PARIS RUNWAYS.

SHISEIDO

RED MADNESS
BY SERGE LUTENS

Available at Nordstrom, to order, call 1-800-7-BEAUTE

Keep it simple, specific, and concise. A basic rule of producing good copy. Each of these ads provides a quick and to the point message about the perfect lip color. But what will draw the reader to one product or ad over the other?

Chanel is "Introducing Lip Intensities" that are hot off the Paris runways. But, what does the copy "Lip colour comes out to play mean"? The visual does feature the lip color box with the "four fabulous finishes and cool colour", but it does not project the "play" concept. In this case, it is probably the strong brand identity that will draw the reader's attention.

The imagery of the made-up red and white harlequin suggests elegant perfection with a touch of "Red Madness" humor — champagne included. This is a very unique image to help differentiate Serge Lutens from its competition.

PRESCRIPTIVES The Plastics

LIP LACQUERS IN YOUR EXACT COLOR. AVAILABLE EXCLUSIVELY AT BERGDORF GOODMAN, NEIMAN MARCUS AND NORDSTROM.

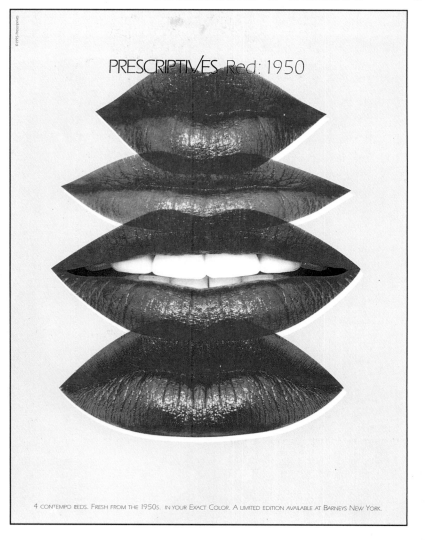

To celebrate — and sell — all of the reds in the lip color spectrum, what better visual than the perfect lips — one pair with all four colors featured or four lips with a stronger image of each color. Prescriptives is offering their key product benefit — "In your exact color".

Some ads featuring specific product benefits and a creative theme will need to provide more information. Max Factor chooses the Hollywood Film Star tie-in with movie "Pretty Woman" and its makeup director, Bob Mills. This ad sells the brand "The Makeup that Performs — Max Factor" and their long-lasting, lipsticks in 36 moisture rich colors.

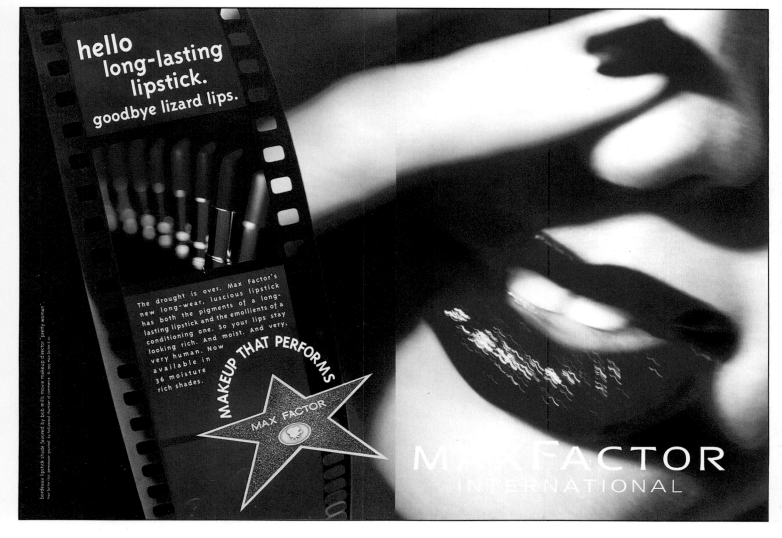

Georgianna is wearing Colour Riche Lipcolour and Nail Enamel in Zinnia, New Blushesse Endless Colour Powder Blush in Cherie and Soft Effects Eyecolour in Mahogany. ©1994 COSMAIR, INC.

Upsy Daisy

Suddenly the world

is colour wonderful.

Shake

everything up.

Kiss convention goodbye.

Please do

pick the roses.

Take license with pink.

Perfect time to turn

the world upside down,

don't you think?

L'ORÉAL

More

Beautiful

By

Design

Three drugstore brands, L'Oreal, Maybelline, and Cutex make a strong case for presenting the product's benefits as they reflect the personal positioning of the customer.

L'Oreal targets the customer who likes to "Shake everything up," and "Kiss convention goodbye"... The gaze motion flows well left to right — with the model's eyes looking at the product as they flow "Upsy Daisy" on down through the copy. The visual/verbal coherence provides a clear, simple, fun message about the product and the consumer.

One of the most clever campaigns with a great play on words is Maybelline's — "Maybe She's Born with It. Maybe It's Maybelline." This is the age old question of how a woman looks so natural — Is it with or without her makeup? Does she look that good in the morning? It is hard for any woman to not ask this question. Whether she will buy Maybelline to achieve that look is another question.

"Color Quick" provides the benefit in the product name. With one simple line of copy and a footnote, Cutex presents the timesaving information the consumer is looking for in home nail care. The graphics are as quick as the message and product benefit. The additional selling point of a wide variety of hot colors is displayed visually.

OPENING NIGHT SENSATION.

She makes something happen wherever she goes. So colorful, so vibrant. Seems like she was meant for the spotlight.

MAYBE SHE'S BORN WITH IT.

MAYBE IT'S **MAYBELLINE.**™

COLOR THAT PERFORMS.

Pampering color bathes lips in moisture. Keratin A helps strengthen nails. Shades go from subtle to bold. Shine on, shine on.

SHADES OF YOU™ **LIPS AND NAILS**

by Maybelline®

By the time you get to your pinky, your thumb is dry!

New COLOR QUICK™ from Cutex. Dries in half—yes, half!—the time of regular nail polish. Hot colors. Glycerine conditioners. Only from Cutex.

CUTEX

combination skin? get even.

introducing
max factor's new balancing act
makeup for a consistent, even finish.

its unique formulation contains both oil-free moisturizers
to prevent dryness and oil-absorbing powders to prevent
shine. it's the makeup that makes up for combination skin.

MAKEUP THAT PERFORMS

MAX FACTOR
INTERNATIONAL

Max Factor effectively introduces its "Balancing Act" foundation with the tie-in to Hollywood movie makeup director Allen Weisinger, for the "Age Of Innocence". This campaign associates its products with the great images of specific movies. This projects quality by an association with the beautiful people that is understood by and/or desired by many women.

The two mascara ads introduce the most desired benefits — "lifts and separates" and "stretch it to the limit" — length. Technology plays a role in Maybelline's new "Clean Brush System". All three ad spreads combine beauty shots with their product shots.

The Maybelline ad is a wonderful play on words and double meanings. The headline is arresting and draws the reader through the copy to the punch line — "Now who needs falsies?" The visual and verbal messages play well together and are definitely on strategy.

Building brand character requires a well conceived strategy that delivers a quality product, communicates a consistent message about the product and consumer benefits, and reflects the values of the brand that are relevant and significant to the target consumer.

These criteria are fully carried out in this "Oil of Olay" campaign. The headline/slogan "A lifetime of beautiful skin." — is illustrated by a range of real people with believable testimonials. The skin treatment products are given a performance feature tag — "What Works". A very clever and convincing lead-in to the copy. It is personal, informal and connects well with the audience.

Many have asked: "How much copy should there be in an ad?" The standard professional answer is — "As much as is necessary to get the message across, simply and clearly." Again, this campaign does it just right. It combines a consistent, strong headline, with what resembles the featured person's handwriting to get the reader's attention and provide a reason to read the ad. It offers solutions to the consumer's problems with product benefits detailed simply in the body copy. The white space gives a clean feeling of freshness.

To complete the "sale", the marketing and communications strategy includes offering the customer a personalized skin care program by calling 1-800-OLAY-4-YOU. Oil of Olay successfully speaks with one voice to its target consumers — from product — to advertising — to customer service.

OIL of **OLAY.** *A lifetime of beautiful skin.*

*Beauty? It's your spirit.
Your intelligence.
They naturally improve
with age. Other things
take a little more work.*

Gabrielle Von Canal, 50,
Documentary Film Maker

What works: Gabrielle uses Beauty Fluid.
Sheer. Light. It quickly penetrates to boost skin's own
moisture renewal process, reducing the look of fine lines and
wrinkles. Every day. We also suggest Facial Cleansing Lotion. Gentle.
Thorough. It leaves skin soft. Not greasy. And Night of Olay. Overnight an
intensive moisture treatment firms and replenishes while you rest.
For your personalized skin care program, please call 1-800-OLAY-4-YOU.

OIL of **OLAY.** *A lifetime of beautiful skin.*

*I don't worry about what
I'm gonna look like
when I'm 40. I worry about
what I'm gonna look like
Friday night.*

Lauren Petty, 15,
High School Student

What works: Lauren uses Fooming Face Wash. 100%
soap-free. 100% oil-free. And light Olay moisture. So your
face feels fresh. Every time you wash it. We also suggest
Oil-Free Beauty Fluid. Not greasy. Not oily. Dermatologist
tested. Won't clog pores. And Refreshing Toner. Clean. Fresh. Cool.
For your personalized skin care program, please call 1-800-OLAY-4-YOU.

Maybe the *secrets of the universe* are not in your immediate

future, but good news, smoother, younger-looking skin is.

How immediate? Like run to the mirror *now,* put on Avon's

new FACE LIFTING *Moisture Firm Foundation.* "Hey, is

that me or my younger sister?"

Honestly... it actually improves the

quality of your skin's appearance.

It feels FIRMER, looks radiant.

You'll get *flawless,* natural-

looking coverage in a lightweight

foundation that's drop-dead gorgeous. You'll see the

difference right away, or your money back. It's kind of like

a FOUNDATION that *thinks it's a face lift.* (Minus the

unexplained thousands missing from your checking account.)

You *will* **discover** the **secret** to *firmer* looking skin. It will appear as a **FOUNDATION.**

© 1996 Avon Products, Inc.

Avon FACE LIFTING
Moisture *Firm* Foundation

FACE LIFTING
MOISTURE FIRM FOUNDATION

Avon

{Call your Avon Representative or 1-800-FOR-AVON.

If you're not happy with your skin, try Starting Over.®

Starting Over
To see new skin each day.
When skin shows lines, flaky
patches, sun damage or uneven
texture, what you are looking at are
worn-out cells that have settled down
on skin's surface. Beneath that dreary
facade is a fresh, healthy-looking
complexion waiting to surface.
You won't have to wait long to see it,
a day or two tops, as a special blend of
nature's own alpha hydroxy acids gently
speeds old layers on their way while
Vitamin A signals new skin to rise up.
Lines retreat, damage fades and
skin shows a smoother,
more radiant surface each day.

ORIGINS
Beauty begins
with your well-being.™

The evolution of man and woman has lead us down the scientific path of discovery. We have discovered numerous ways to make us think we can look younger than our years. Whether anyone really believes this is possible is irrelevant to the producers of skin treatment products because they know that nearly everyone in a "civilized society" wants to look as young and fresh-faced as possible.

These four ads speak to that need in women. From Avon's crystal ball "secrets of the universe," to Origins Starting Over "new skin each day," to Prescriptives "scientific firming complex," and Oil of Olay's "Visible Recovery" — we are being offered a wide variety of products to give us the "fountain of youth".

Seriously, the ads themselves do present their products convincingly. Each positions itself to offer solutions — to either firmer, smoother, fresher or newer skin. Avon has combined its "Face Lifting" lotion in a "Moisture Firm Foundation". The Origins' campaign has a simple, direct "message in a bottle". As a retailer, Neiman Marcus is presenting its exclusivity with Prescriptives' Extra Firm cream. Oil of Olay presents its New Hydroxy Discovery.

Note the different layout and design choices. Two ads chose to show only the packaged product in single page ads. Two have used beauty shots in double page spreads. The Oil of Olay ad has strategically used a layer of velum film pulled back to visually communicate the message given in the headline and body copy.

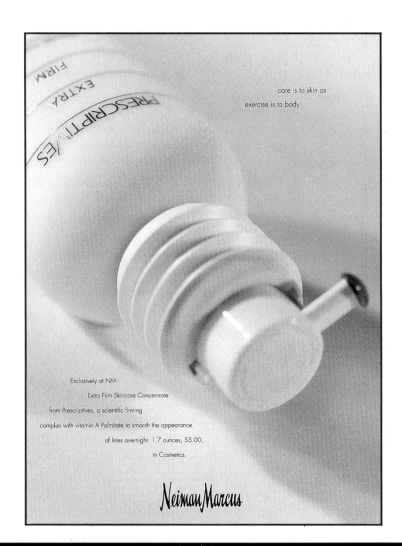

care is to skin as
exercise is to body.

Exclusively at NM:

Extra Firm Skincare Concentrate

from Prescriptives, a scientific firming

complex with vitamin A Palmitate to smooth the appearance

of lines overnight. 1.7 ounces, 55.00,

in Cosmetics.

NeimanMarcus

NEW HYDROXY

Now find clearer, younger looking skin. Right beneath the skin you have.

Discover Oil of Olay Hydroxy
Renewal Cream, our Dual-Action
Hydroxy Complex.

Exfoliating: Our hydroxy compound
exfoliates dull, dry surface skin that can
make you look older. Uncovering newer,
more radiant skin.
Hydrating: Olay moisture hydrates
newly revealed skin.
The Results: **Improved skin clarity.
The look of fine lines and wrinkles
visibly reduced.**

OIL OF OLAY
RENEWAL CREAM
VISIBLE RECOVERY
SERIES

DISCOVERY

ULTRESS N° 35

"MAKE HIM DROP THE REMOTE CONTROL" RED

Revel in the world's only haircolor with luminescent gel. Ultress. For color that's deeply vibrant. Endlessly rich. And so gloriously seductive, he just might lose total control.

GORGEOUS HAIR IS THE BEST REVENGE.

CLAIROL

ULTRESS N° 16

"SUPER BOWL? WHAT SUPER BOWL?" BLONDE

Revel in the world's only haircolor with luminescent gel.
And feel the power of color.

ULTRESS
CLAIROL

ULTRESS N° 50

"BLONDES DON'T HAVE MORE FUN" BRUNETTE

Revel in the world's only haircolor with luminescent gel.
And feel the power of color.

ULTRESS
CLAIROL

One thing certain about the American consumer, we have very diverse values, attitudes, and lifestyles. Advertisers spend time and money on extensive research to understand the various target markets.

Some women (known fondly as feminists) may object to the Clairol campaign that presents these women as living solely for their men. What is the meaning of the message: "And feel the power of color"? For the woman who needs to "control her man" the product name might be "temptress" rather than "Ultress".

There are other women who seek to pamper themselves in order to "invigorate their senses" internally and externally. Organic Moods' ads have been designed to provide visual feelings of "Energy. Tranquility. Harmony.", which is their slogan. They have chosen a layout design that literally puts the product in the mind of the consumer — note the product photo insert superimposed over the head of the model. The imagery in the photo tells the whole "mood enhancing" story. The photography is so real, you can feel the heat of the sun on your skin and the water on your face. This puts the reader in the mood for these products and this brand.

On page 158 — Redken's campaign for their hair care products uses a similar, clean layout like the previously discussed Oil of Olay campaign on pages 152-153. Once again, the product is presented as a solution to everyday, real problems. But the approach here is much more of a 90's message, as opposed to the Clairol campaign on page 156. The target consumers are obviously coming from very different lifestyles and attitudes.

working out makes your hair exhausted.

it might be an excuse not to
work out, but before you get
carried away, consider this.

chlorine can damage your hair,
and too much washing and
blowdrying only make it worse.
one 2 one, the new personal
care system from redken,
can help. its vitamin-mineral-
protein complex locks a
protective layer of protein
to the hair and creates
a kind of buffer between your
hair and what's damaging it.
we're not saying it's going to
motivate you to climb another
set of stairs. but at least
you won't have to worry
about your hair.

○ sun ○ diet ○ pollution ● exercise

the full line of one 2 one
for the hair, skin and body is
available only in salons. so
ask your stylist for it. or for
the nearest redken salon
call 1-800-REDKEN-8.

to preserve and protect. One 2 One

REDKEN
5TH AVENUE NYC

did you eat something bad for your hair today?

who knows? you can't worry
about every little thing you eat
and the effect it's going
to have on you.

but you can do a little
preventive maintenance on
the outside. one 2 one is a
new personal care system
from redken featuring
a vitamin-mineral-protein
complex that locks a protective
layer of protein to the hair.
we're not saying that using this
gives you license to eat
whatever you want. but it will
give you great looking hair.

○ sun ● diet ○ pollution ○ exercise

the full line of one 2 one
for the hair, skin and body is
available only in salons. so
ask your stylist for it. or for
the nearest redken salon
call 1-800-REDKEN-8.

to preserve and protect. One 2 One

REDKEN
5TH AVENUE NYC

$\mathcal{K}$ey Terms

used in

What Works in Fashion Advertising

- *Objectives* are what the advertiser wants to attain and what response (quantitative and/or qualitative) is desired.

- The *strategy* must fit the objective. It is the core of the message and how it will be conveyed in terms of its meanings to the consumer.

- Meanings may include *product benefits, consumer benefits, promises, solutions, comparisons, idealizations...*

- *Tactics* are creative elements that execute the message with impact. Copywriters and art directors create ideas that are called *tactics* or *executions* that can ideally convey the strategy.

- *Tone* involves the "voice" and style of the message based on the frame of reference of the audience.

- *Brand character* describes the most significant values and attributes of the brand to the consumer. Benefits are expressed in language that best personify and dramatize the intrinsic values of the brand.

- *Themes* come from researched information about consumer behavior and from usage data about products and brands. Themes are based on consumer knowledge that can be used to differentiate the product from its competition.

- Strategic *positioning* gives the advertiser "ownership" of market. Creating unique perceptions about a brand help it gain a niche in the mind of the consumer. This is called positioning against the competition.

- *Being on strategy* means that your objectives, tactics, and tone are relevant and appealing to the target consumer.